Tropical Houses

Tropical Houses

teNeues

Editor in chief: Paco Asensio

Project coordination and texts: Cynthia Reschke

Editorial coordination: Haike Falkenberg

Art director: Mireia Casanovas Soley

Layout: Gisela Legares Gili

Copy-editing: Raquel Vicente Durán

English translation: Robert J. Nusbaum

French translation: Marion Westerhoff, Christine Belakhdar

Spanish translation: Almudena Sasiain

Published by teNeues Publishing Group

teNeues Publishing Company
16 West 22nd Street, New York, NY 10010, US
Tel.: 001-212-627-9090, Fax: 001-212-627-9511

teNeues Book Division
Kaistraße 18
40221 Düsseldorf, Germany
Tel.: 0049-(0)211-994597-0, Fax: 0049-(0)211-994597-40

teNeues Publishing UK Ltd.
P.O. Box 402
West Byfleet
KT14 7ZF, Great Britain
Tel.: 0044-1932-403509, Fax: 0044-1932-403514

www.teneues.com

ISBN: 3-8238-4544-6

Editorial project: © 2003 LOFT Publications

Via Laietana 32, 4º Of. 92
08003 Barcelona, Spain
Tel.: 0034 932 688 088
Fax: 0034 932 687 073

e-mail: loft@loftpublications.com
www.loftpublications.com

Printed by: Gràfiques Iberia, S.A. Spain
August 2003

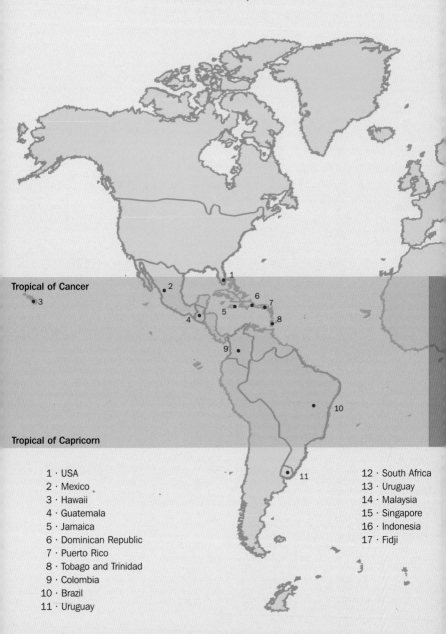

Western Hemisphere

Tropical of Cancer

Tropical of Capricorn

1 · USA
2 · Mexico
3 · Hawaii
4 · Guatemala
5 · Jamaica
6 · Dominican Republic
7 · Puerto Rico
8 · Tobago and Trinidad
9 · Colombia
10 · Brazil
11 · Uruguay

12 · South Africa
13 · Uruguay
14 · Malaysia
15 · Singapore
16 · Indonesia
17 · Fidji

Introduction

Paradise-like and enchanting islands in places like the Caribbean, South Pacific and other parts of the limitless expanse of the ocean; endless lonely beaches, tropical vegetation with exotic flowers, banana trees, coconut palms and mango trees, and glorious sunrises and sunsets featuring painterly colors on the horizon and sea: these are all images of the tropic that people throughout the world dream of. Joie de vivre, harmony, passion and creativity are part and parcel of everyday life in these regions where the clock seems to move slower: a world where one can enjoy the pleasures of the senses in every sense of the term. And regardless of whatever advantages and disadvantages may accrue to life in the tropics, what is special about life in these regions is that people are much more exposed to the violence of nature and at the same time closer to nature.

Tropical regions are found everywhere on the planet, from the Tropic of Cancer to the Tropic of Capricorn. Africa is the only continent that almost completely spans these two regions although parts of Asia, Australia, the Oceanic region, a small section of the U.S., all of Central America and much of South America are also located in tropical regions, which cover approximately 40 percent of the Earth's surface and are home to about half of the world's population. The geotopography of tropical regions tends to be rather extreme on the various continents, for here you find the highest mountains (parts of the Andes, the African highlands, the mountains of New Guinea), the longest rivers (the Nile, Amazon, Congo and Ganges) and the deepest ocean floors. Tropical rainforests are home to an astonishing variety of species of flora and

fauna that is unmatched on earth: orchid and fruit tree blossoms create splotches of glorious color amidst the lush green of the jungle, sharing their habitats with frogs, parrots and countless other animal species.

The inhabitants of hot and humid climates prefer spending much of their time out of doors. This lifestyle is reflected in most tropical buildings, which are replete with open verandas, living rooms and dining rooms that allow gardens and the natural landscape to blend into each other and to extend seamlessly to the house itself, creating a healthy synergy between the natural and human habitats. Cultural life is also strongly reflected in the architectural design of these regions where every home is a work of art and every homeowner an artist. For generations now, inhabitants of tropical regions have proudly produced work in wood, stone, fabric, bamboo, ceramic, mussel shells, batik and embroidery. Most materials come from the immediate environs and much is created from limited resources.

The key elements of tropical architecture are light, air and water. Nature's ways are respected, but she is also used wisely as a shield against her extremes such as intense heat and torrential rains. For example, while the sun is the source of all light, tropical architecture is known for creating cool, shady and well ventilated spaces that provide shelter from the intense heat of the fireball above. It is for this reason that walls are often eschewed in tropical homes and that a maximum number of openings are created so as to admit as much air as possible into the house. Thus, open

spaces with roofs projecting far out over them are a basic element in tropical architecture, most of whose elements are determined by the climate. Such projecting roofs, which are generally made of wood, create a shadowy environment of soothing dimness. This half-light establishes tropical architecture as a form in its own right, rather than as just an outgrowth of the necessity to block out the sun and the elements. Tropical architecture uses pergolas and projecting roofs to create gentle transitions between the relentless tropical sun outside and the soothing semi-darkness within what are often wood palaces. These overhanging structures are often cascaded and are supported by long beams and high wooden posts. The roofs of these houses are also outfitted with ingenious slit configurations in their gables and ventilation systems in their roofs that channel air inside. Doors, walls and other elements can be manually adjusted to optimize air flow according to wind direction. The ventilation systems in tropical houses are so well designed that air conditioning is needless.

In some homes, roof decks keep the spaces beneath them comfortably cool and at the same time integrate the natural environment into the house. These unique traditional structures are often built in a horseshoe shape around a swimming pool where the residents can gather and enjoy the refreshing coolness. Sometimes large pools are located alongside the outer walls of the house, cooling the warm air before it has a chance to enter the house. Dwellings perched on three-foot stilts are cooled by natural ventilation from beneath, an architectural strategy which also minimizes their impact on the natural environment by preventing the

entire mass of the house from pressing down on the earth. This is also beneficial in that the damp and muddy terrain created by torrential tropical rains is kept at bay. Highly resistant tropical construction materials, mainly wood, provide excellent protection against the elements and are in keeping with regional aesthetic and architectural traditions.

All of these architectural principles, practices and techniques are of a piece: the harmony between the materials used and the natural environment and the enchanting designs created by architects and builders are consistent with the cultural identity and unique character of tropical regions. To create a comfortable environment in these regions, nothing matters more than blocking out the light, admitting air to the house, decreasing the temperature and thus avoiding humidity and mildew. These are only some of the techniques deployed by architects such as Wijaya Tribwana, Guz architects, Architects Pacific, CSL Associates and Bedmar & Shi.

The homes depicted in this book are of course only a small selection of many fine tropical homes, and by the same token this book only reflects a handful of the multifarious aspects of tropical lifestyles. The places represented here, which include Jamaica, Bali, the Mexican coast, Hawaii, Indonesia, Thailand, Malaysia, Brazil and Fiji, are divided into two sections according to whether they are located in the Eastern or Western hemispheres. Thus, one section contains houses from North, Central and South America while the remaining houses are from Africa, Asia and the Oceanic region.

Einleitung

Paradiesische und magische Inselwelten in der Karibik, der Südsee und anderen Teilen der grenzenlosen Weiten der Ozeane, unendlich lange verlassene Strände, tropische Vegetation mit exotischen Blumen, Bananenstauden, Kokospalmen und Mangobäume, traumhafte Sonnenauf- und untergänge mit malerischen Farbspielen am Horizont und auf dem Wasser – all dies sind Bilder, die Menschen aus allen Teilen der Welt von den Tropen träumen lassen. Lebensfreude und Harmonie, Leidenschaft und Kreativität sind hier an der Tagesordnung, wo die Uhr langsamer zu ticken scheint – eine Welt sinnlicher Erfahrung in jeder Beziehung. Neben allen Vor- und Nachteilen ist das Besondere am Leben in den Tropen, dass der Mensch den Naturgewalten viel mehr ausgesetzt ist und der Natur dadurch auch viel mehr verbunden ist.

Die Tropen umspannen den gesamten Globus und erstrecken sich zwischen dem Wendekreis des Krebses und dem Wendekreis des Steinbocks. Afrika ist der einzige Kontinent, der fast komplett zwischen diesen beiden Breitengraden liegt. Aber auch Teile von Asien, Australien, Ozeanien, ein kleiner Teil der Vereinigten Staaten, ganz Mittelamerika und ein Großteil Südamerikas befinden sich auf diesem Erdstrich. Sie decken ungefähr 40% der Erdoberfläche ab und etwa die Hälfte der Weltbevölkerung lebt hier. Extreme Bedingungen charakterisieren diese Teile der Erde auf den unterschiedlichen Kontinenten – die höchsten Berge (Teile der Anden, das afrikanische Hochland, die Berge von Neu Guinea), die größten Flüsse (Nil, Amazonas, Kongo, Ganges) sowie die tiefsten ozeanischen Gräben. Im Regenwald gedeiht die größte Vielfalt an Flora in Bezug auf die Anzahl unterschiedlicher

Spezies und auch das Tierreich ist mannigfaltig und artenreich wie sonst nirgendwo auf der Erde – Blüten von Orchideen und Obstbäumen zeichnen bunte Farbtupfer in das saftige Grün und teilen sich ihren Lebensraum mit Fröschen, Papageien und vielen anderen Geschöpfen.

Bei warm-feuchtem Klima lebt man am liebsten im Freien. So ist bei den meisten Gebäuden eine große offene Veranda Wohn- und Esszimmer zugleich. Hier fließen Landschaft und Garten wie ein Gemälde zusammen und reichen übergangslos bis ins Haus hinein, sodass Natur und menschlicher Lebensraum eine Symbiose bilden. Auch kulturelle Aspekte spiegeln sich stark wider im Design, jeder hier ist ein Künstler, beherrscht ein Handwerk. Seit Generationen ist man stolz auf sorgfältig angefertigte Arbeiten aus Holz, Stein, Stoff, Bambus, Keramik, Muschelsplittern, stolz auf Batik-, Stickereiarbeiten und vieles mehr. Die verwendeten Materialien stammen meistens aus der nächsten Umgebung und aus Wenig wird Viel gemacht.

Licht, Luft und Wasser sind fundamentale Elemente in der tropischen Architektur. Die Natur wird außerordentlich respektiert und gleichzeitig auch genutzt, um sich gegen ihre Gewalten wie Hitze oder starke Regenfälle zu schützen. Die Sonne ist zum Beispiel eine wertvolle Lichtquelle, doch der geschätzte Schatten kennzeichnet die tropische Architektur mehr als das warme Licht des Feuerballs, dessen Hitzeeinwirkung mittels Schatten und Ventilation neutralisiert werden soll. Aus diesem Grund werden Wände oft aus dem tropischen Baukonzept entfernt und es

werden so viele Öffnungen wie möglich geschaffen, um der Luft freie Bahn zu gewähren. Solche offenen Räume mit großen, weit überhängenden Dächern, gelten als elementare Faktoren dieser vom Klima geprägten Baukunst. Unter den in der Regel aus Holz konstruierten Dächern wohnen Tiefe, Reflexion und das Halbdunkel, das den Schatten ausmacht. Dieses Halbdunkel ist eine Möglichkeit, die tropische Architektur jenseits des traditionellen (Sonnen-)Schirms als eigenständige Architekturform anzuerkennen – es ist der Übergang des intensiven rohen Lichts von Außen hin zum Dämmerlicht im Herzen der Holzschlösser, hervorgerufen und gefiltert durch Dachvorsprünge und Pergolas. Diese sind häufig kaskadenförmig angeordnet, gestützt auf lange Balken und hohe Pfähle. Zusammen mit geschickt angebrachten lamellenartigen Schlitzen in den Dachgiebeln sowie Zuluft- und Abluftdächern lenken sie den Luftstrom. Anhand manuell verstellbarer Türen, Wände und anderer Elemente kann der Durchzug optimal geregelt werden, je nachdem aus welcher Himmelsrichtung der Wind bläst. Die gesamte Konstruktion ist so perfektioniert, dass eine herkömmliche Klimaanlage überflüssig wird.

Des weiteren kühlen angelegte Dachterrassen die darunter liegenden Bereiche und bringen zugleich ein Stückchen Natur ins Haus. Die einzigartigen traditionellen Bauten sind oft in U-Form um den Swimming Pool herum gebaut, an dem man zusammenkommen und sich erfrischen kann. Oder aber die großen Becken winden sich direkt an der Hauswand entlang, sodass die heiße Luft erst durch das Wasser abgekühlt wird, bevor sie in das Haus eindringt. Etwa einen Meter vom Erdboden aufgeständerte Häuser profitieren von natürlicher Belüftung von unten und gewährleisten

zugleich einen minimalen Eingriff in die geschätzte Natur, da der Boden nicht durch das gesamte Volumen des Hauses erdrückt wird – und bei starken Regenfällen bieten sie einen vorteilhaften und sicheren Abstand zum nassen, schlammigen Erdboden. Widerstandsfähige tropische Baumaterialien, vorwiegend regionale Hölzer, bürgen für witterungsgerechte und zugleich ästhetisch schöne traditionelle Bauten.

Diese Prinzipien und Verfahren gehen alle Hand in Hand – der Einklang von verwendeten Materialien mit der Natur und den Zauberformeln der Baumeister erfüllt alle Merkmale der tropischen Architektur mit ihrer kulturellen Identität und einzigartigem Charakter. Um eine angenehme Atmosphäre zu schaffen, ist es also wichtig das Licht zu dämmen, der Luft Eintritt zu gewähren, die Temperatur zu senken und dadurch Feuchtigkeit und Schimmelbildung zu vermeiden. Dies sind nur einige der Tricks von Baukünstlern dieser Breiten wie Wijaya Tribwana, Guz architects, Architects Pacific, CSL Associates oder Bedmar & Shi.

Selbstverständlich kann auf den folgenden Seiten nur eine Auslese vorgestellt werden und es wird nur ein Teil aller Facetten der tropischen Lebensweise widergespiegelt. Die Auswahl aus Ländern wie Jamaika, Bali, den Küsten Mexikos, Hawaii, Indonesien, Thailand, Malaysien, Brasilien oder Fidschi wird in diesem Buch in zwei Kapitel gefasst, wobei unser Planet ausgehend vom Nullmeridian in die linke und die rechte Erdhälfte geteilt wird. Ein Kapitel präsentiert Entwürfe aus Nord- Mittel- und Südamerika, der zweite Teil umfasst Afrika, Asien und Ozeanien.

Introduction

Monde paradisiaque et magique des îles des Caraïbes, des mers du sud et autres recoins de l'horizon illimité de l'océan, longues plages vierges à l'infini, végétation tropicale aux fleurs exotiques, bananiers, cocotiers et manguiers, merveilleux couchers et levers de soleil – colorant l'eau et l'horizon de jeux de lumières pittoresques – autant d'images, qui font rêver des tropiques, les hommes de tous les coins de la planète. Joie de vivre et harmonie, passion et créativité sont à l'ordre du jour, là où le temps semble s'écouler plus lentement – un monde sensuel dans tous les sens du terme. La vie dans les tropiques, avantages et inconvénients mis à part, est tout à fait singulière. En effet, la soumission de l'homme à la force des éléments naturels implique une union beaucoup plus étroite avec la nature.

Les tropiques font le tour du globe et s'étendent entre le tropique du cancer et le tropique du capricorne. L'Afrique est le seul continent presque entièrement compris entre ces deux degrés de latitude. Certaines régions de l'Asie, l'Australie, l'Océanie, une petite partie des Etats-Unis, toute l'Amérique Centrale et la plupart de l'Amérique du Sud sont sous les tropiques. Ils couvrent à peu près 40% de la superficie terrestre et accueillent environ la moitié de la population mondiale. Des conditions extrêmes caractérisent ces parties de la Terre sur les différents continents – on y trouve les plus hauts sommets (une partie des Andes, le haut-plateau africain, les montagnes de Nouvelle Guinée), les plus grands fleuves (Nil, Amazone, Kongo, Ganges) ainsi que les fosses océanes les plus profondes. La forêt tropicale abrite la plus grande variété d'espèces animales et végétales comme nulle part ailleurs sur la

Terre – fleurs d'orchidées et d'arbres fruitiers dessinent des touches de couleurs sur le vert éclatant et se partagent l'espace vital avec grenouilles, perroquets et maintes autres créatures.

Sous un climat chaud et humide, on préfère vivre dehors. La plupart des habitations ont donc une véranda profonde et ouverte, servant à la fois de séjour et salle à manger. Comme sur un tableau, paysage et nature se mêlent et pénètrent dans la maison pour former une symbiose entre la nature et l'espace vital de l'homme. Les aspects culturels se reflètent aussi fortement dans le design : ici tout le monde est artiste ou artisan. De générations en générations, on est fier de fabriquer de jolis objets de bois, pierre, tissus, bambous, céramique, éclats de coquillages, fier des ouvrages en batik, des broderies et plus encore. On utilise souvent les matières de source locale : avec peu de chose, on fait beaucoup.

La lumière, l'air et l'eau sont les caractéristiques fondamentales de l'architecture tropicale. Elle respecte tout particulièrement la nature et l'utilise à la fois pour se protéger contre sa violence, lors de fortes chaleurs ou de pluies torrentielles. Le soleil, par exemple, est une source de lumière précieuse, pourtant l'ombre caractérise davantage l'architecture tropicale que la chaleur du rayonnement de cette boule de feu, dont on neutralise les effets thermiques grâce à l'ombre et à la ventilation. C'est pourquoi, la conception de l'architecture tropicale est de décloisonner l'espace afin de créer un plus grand nombre d'ouvertures, laissant ainsi circuler l'air librement : pièces ouvertes protégées par de larges avancées de toitures, sont les qualités élémentaires de cet art de

la construction. Les toits, construits le plus souvent en bois, abritent profondeur, réflexion et pénombre, génératrices d'ombre. Ce demi-jour est un concept propre à l'architecture tropicale, et s'ajoute à l'idée architecturale traditionnelle d'effet (pare)-soleil – c'est le passage de la lumière crue et intense de l'extérieur vers la pénombre au cœur des châteaux de bois, engendrée et filtrée par de larges avancées de toitures et grandes pergolas. Souvent agencées en cascade, elles sont soutenues par des poutres et pilotis élevés. Ces éléments permettent de guider les traversées d'air grâce à des fentes en forme de lamelles judicieusement placées dans le pignon ou à des ouïes d'entrée et de sorties d'air dans les toits. Portes, cloisons et autres éléments ajustables manuellement permettent un réglage parfait de la ventilation, selon le sens où le vent souffle. La perfection d'un tel système de ventilation permet de se passer de l'air conditionné habituel.

Les terrasses de toit rafraîchissent les zones inférieures tout en faisant entrer la nature dans la maison. Les constructions traditionnelles et originales sont souvent en forme de U et bâties autour de la piscine, où l'on peut se réunir et se rafraîchir. Les grands bassins sont également implantés directement le long du mur de l'habitation pour que l'eau refroidisse l'air chaud avant qu'il ne pénètre à l'intérieur. Construites à environ un mètre au-dessus du sol, les maisons profitent d'une ventilation naturelle par le bas. Ce type de construction minimalise l'atteinte faite à la nature car le terrain n'est pas complètement écrasé sous le volume de la maison. En outre, lors de pluies torrentielles, il assure

une distance qui protège du terrain humide et boueux. Matériaux tropicaux résistants, notamment essences de bois locaux; permettent de construire de belles maisons traditionnelles, adaptées aux conditions météorologiques.

Ces principes et procédés vont de pair – l'harmonie entre matériaux utilisés, nature et formules magiques du maître d'œuvre donne à l'architecture tropicale toutes les caractéristiques qui lui confèrent identité culturelle et nature unique. Pour créer une atmosphère agréable, il est donc important de tamiser la lumière, d'assurer la circulation de l'air, de baisser la température afin d'éviter la formation d'humidité et de moisissures. Ce ne sont que quelques-unes des astuces de ces artistes de la construction tropicale tels Wijaya Tribwana, Guz architects, Architects Pacific, CSL Associates ou Bedmar & Shi.

Il est bien évident que les pages suivantes ne peuvent offrir qu'une sélection d'œuvres, quelques reflets de toutes les facettes de l'art de vivre sous les tropiques. Les projets choisis, situés dans les pays à droite et à gauche des deux hémisphères de la planète, à partir du méridien zéro, – Jamaïque, Bali, côtes du Mexique, Hawaï, Indonésie, Thaïlande, Malaisie, Brésil ou îles Fidji – sont répartis, dans ce livre, en deux chapitres. Le premier comprend l'Amérique du Nord, du Sud et Centrale, le deuxième embrasse l'Afrique, l'Asie et l'Océanie.

Introducción

El mundo paradisiaco y mágico de las islas del Caribe, de los mares del sur y otros rincones de los inconmensurables océanos; las playas desiertas sin fin; la vegetación tropical de exóticas flores, bananeros, cocoteros y mangos; amaneceres y puestas de sol de ensueño con juegos de luces de postal reflejados en el horizonte sobre las aguas; son estas imágenes las que hacen soñar a gente de todo el mundo con los trópicos. La alegría y la armonía, la pasión y la creatividad están constantemente presentes en este lugar, donde el reloj parece marcar las horas lentamente; un mundo sensual en el más amplio sentido de la palabra. Con todas las ventajas y desventajas que ello conlleva, la peculiaridad de la vida en el trópico consiste, principalmente, en que la población está mucho más expuesta a las fuerzas de la naturaleza y, por tanto, mucho más unida a ella.

Los trópicos circunvalan todo el globo y se extienden, de ahí su nombre, entre el trópico de cáncer y el trópico de capricornio. África es el único continente situado casi por completo en estas latitudes, pero también zonas de Asia, Australia, Oceanía, una pequeña región de Estados Unidos, toda Centroamérica y grandes áreas de Sudamérica se encuentran en ellas. Las regiones tropicales abarcan aproximadamente el 40% de la superficie terrestre y acogen cerca de la mitad de la población mundial. Condiciones meteorológicas y orográficas extremas caracterizan esta parte de la Tierra repartida entre los diversos continentes – las montañas más altas (algunos picos de los Andes, las tierras altas africanas, las montañas de Nueva Guinea), los ríos más caudalosos (el Nilo, el Amazonas, el Congo, el Ganges), así como las fosas abisales

más profundas. En sus selvas crece la flora más rica en lo que a número de especies se refiere, y el reino animal resulta magnífico y variado como en ningún otro sitio del planeta; los capullos de las orquídeas y de los frutales lucen todo su colorido sobre el intenso verde y comparten hábitat con ranas, papagayos y otras extraordinarias criaturas.

En este clima cálido y húmedo la vida se traslada al exterior. Así, la mayoría de los edificios tienen una veranda abierta que sirve de comedor y sala de estar. El paisaje se funde con el jardín en un único espacio y penetra directamente en la casa, de forma que la naturaleza y el ser humano forman una simbiosis. También los aspectos culturales se reflejan con intensidad en el diseño: cualquiera es aquí un artista, cualquiera domina la artesanía. Desde hace generaciones, se llevan a cabo trabajos en madera, piedra, tela, bambú, cerámica, conchas, técnicas de estampado de telas, bordados y muchos más, de los cuales están orgullosos. Los materiales que se utilizan proceden casi siempre del entorno más inmediato y con medios sencillos se obtienen resultados espectaculares.

La luz, el aire y el agua son elementos fundamentales en la arquitectura tropical. Como en ningún otro lugar, la naturaleza se respeta y al tiempo se utiliza como protección contra el calor o las lluvias torrenciales. Y aunque el sol es una valiosa fuente de luz, la apreciada sombra caracteriza las construcciones tropicales más que los cálidos rayos de la bola de fuego, cuyos efectos hay que neutralizar con ayuda de sombras y ventilación. Por ello, la

supresión de tabiques es habitual en este concepto arquitectónico y se hacen tantas aberturas como resulte posible para crear corrientes de aire. Los espacios abiertos con aleros que sobresalen ampliamente están considerados asimismo un factor elemental en este tipo de casas tan influidas por el clima. Los tejados, por lo general de madera, acogen la profundidad, la reflexión y la penumbra inherentes a la sombra. Esa penumbra proporciona un carácter propio a la arquitectura tropical, más allá de las tradicionales sombrillas, en una transición entre la intensa y cruda luz del exterior y la iluminación crepuscular del corazón de estos palacios de madera; una luz atraída y filtrada a un tiempo por los salientes de los tejaroces y las pérgolas. Estos suelen estar colocados en forma de cascada, apoyados sobre largas vigas y altos postes y, al igual que las hendiduras en forma de láminas abiertas en los aguilones y los tejadillos de ventilación para la entrada y salida adicional del aire, se utilizan para canalizar la corriente de aire. Las puertas, ventanas y otros elementos regulables manualmente pueden reconducir también la ventilación, gracias a de la dirección con la que sople el viento. Estos tipos de métodos están perfeccionados de tal forma que no es necesaria la instalación de aire acondicionado.

Por otro lado, las azoteas y los frescos espacios que quedan debajo de ellas sirven además para dar paso a la naturaleza hacia el interior de las viviendas. Las construcciones tradicionales suelen tener forma de U y se concentran alrededor de una piscina, que a su vez es el lugar de reunión y de ambiente fresco. Las piscinas pueden extenderse también adosadas a lo largo de una

pared de la casa, de forma que el aire caliente se refrigere antes de entrar en las estancias. Las construcciones que se levantan a 1 metro del suelo aprovechan la ventilación natural y apenas interfieren en la naturaleza, ya que no aplastan el suelo con su gran volumen. Además, en caso de lluvias torrenciales, ofrecen distancia y seguridad con respecto al suelo húmedo y a los lodos. Los resistentes materiales tropicales de construcción, sobre todo las maderas locales, crean construcciones que ofrecen gran aislamiento térmico sin dejar de ser bellas y tradicionales.

Estos principios y métodos están vinculados; la armonía de los materiales utilizados con la naturaleza y las fórmulas magistrales de los constructores reflejan todas las características de la arquitectura tropical con su identidad cultural y su particular carácter. Para lograr un ambiente agradable es, por tanto, fundamental suavizar la luz, dejar circular al aire, bajar las temperaturas, y evitar así la humedad y la formación de moho. Estos son solo algunos de los secretos de arquitectos como Wijaya Tribwana, Guz architects, Architects Pacific, CSL Associates o Bedmar & Shi.

Por supuesto, las páginas siguientes solamente recogen una pequeña muestra y una visión parcial de todas las facetas de la vida en el trópico. Los lugares elegidos –Jamaica, Bali, la costa mexicana, Hawai, Indonesia, Tailandia, Malasia, Brasil o Fiji– se recogen en el libro en dos capítulos diferentes, del mismo modo que nuestro planeta azul se divide en dos mitades a ambos lados del meridiano de Greenwich. De esta manera, un capítulo presenta proyectos distribuidos por todo el continente americano, mientras que el otro abarca construcciones situadas en África, Asia y Oceanía.

Western
Hemisphere

Dani's House

Decoration: **By the residents**
Location: **Miami, USA**
Photos: © **José Luis Hausmann**

Though an inveterate globetrotter, surfer and photographer Daniel Balda loves returning home from his travels, not least because he himself built this cozy haven in a huge garden with his own hands—and a little help from a local construction company. The garage was converted into a wispy cottage which contains only a bedroom, dressing room, toilet and sink. The shower is outside. The original garage door was replaced by a sliding glass door with the result that this cozy little dwelling now looks out over the pool. The convivial yard area is the center of household leisure time activity, and right next to it, under a tree, stands a wooden dining room table with matching chairs.

Der Surfer und Fotograf Daniel Balda ist viel auf Reisen und freut sich jedes Mal, in sein gemütliches Heim zurückzukehren. Mit Hilfe einer Baufirma konstruierte er selbst diese kleine Oase inmitten eines großen Gartens. Sie nutzten die Struktur der Garage und verwandelten sie in ein kleines Häuschen mit Schlaf- und Ankleidezimmer, Toilette und Waschbecken. An der Außenseite wurde eine Dusche installiert. Das Garagentor wurde durch eine Glasschiebetür ersetzt und auf den Pool ausgerichtet. Draußen befindet sich ein gemütlicher Aufenthaltsbereich, wo sich die Hauptaktivitäten abspielen. Daneben steht unter einem Baum der Esstisch aus Holz mit passenden Stühlen.

Daniel Balda, surfeur et photographe, voyage beaucoup et à chaque retour, adore retrouver le confort de sa maison. C'est avec une entreprise de construction qu'il construit lui-même cette petite oasis au milieu d'un grand jardin. L'idée : transformer la structure d'un garage en une petite maison comprenant chambre à coucher et dressing, toilettes et coin lavabo, la douche étant fixée à l'extérieur. La porte du garage a été remplacée par une baie vitrée coulissante orientée sur la piscine. L'extérieur offre un très agréable espace à vivre, lieu où se déroulent les activités principales. A côté, la table en bois et les chaises assorties sont installées sous un arbre.

Daniel Balda, surfista y fotógrafo, adora regresar a su acogedor hogar tras sus frecuentes viajes. Con ayuda de una empresa constructora, él mismo levantó este pequeño oasis en medio de un amplio jardín. Para ello utilizó la estructura del garaje y lo convirtió en una casita con un dormitorio, un vestidor y un lavabo. Instaló la ducha en el exterior y sustituyó la puerta del garaje por una de cristal abierta hacia la piscina. El exterior posee una agradable área de estar, en la que se desarrollan las principales actividades cotidianas. Al lado, bajo un árbol, está la mesa de madera con sillas a juego que se utiliza para comer.

House on the Hill

Architect: **Diego Villaseñor**
Location: **Mexico**
Photos: © **Undine Pröhl**

The architecture of this hilltop house dovetails perfectly with the surrounding rocky landscape and natural vegetation. In designing this home, the architect also gave nature her due by incorporating into the inner courtyard an existing tree which, when it blossoms, tints the heart of this home an intense shade of pink. The roof is made of palm branches thatched across a wooden frame. The main common areas, such as a cosy "sitting room", which doubles as a dining area, are located outdoors under a covered terrace. The jacuzzi and hammocks are wonderful venues for relaxing and enjoying the ambience of this lovely home.

Das Haus liegt auf einer Anhöhe und sein Entwurf passt sich ausgezeichnet der steinigen Umgebung und der unberührten Vegetation an. Aus Respekt zur Natur wurde im Innenhof ein Baum erhalten, der zur Blütezeit den Kern des Hauses mit einem kräftigen Rosa färbt. Das Dach ist aus Palmwedeln, die über eine tragende Holzstruktur gelegt sind. Die wichtigsten Aufenthaltsbereiche, wie zum Beispiel eine gemütliche Sitzecke, die einem Wohnzimmer gleicht, und wo man auch die Mahlzeiten zu sich nehmen kann, befinden sich im Freien auf der überdachten Terrasse. Der Whirlpool und die Hängematte sind herrliche Orte zum Entspannen.

La maison située sur une hauteur, est conçue de manière à s'intégrer parfaitement bien au terrain rocailleux et à la nature vierge environnante. Pour respecter la nature, l'architecte a gardé un arbre dans la cour, dont la floraison colorie le cœur de la maison d'un rose vif. Le toit est constitué de branches de palmier, posées sur une structure en bois portante. Les espaces à vivre les plus importants se situent sur la terrasse couverte, à l'air libre, comme le banc d'angle aussi confortable qu'une salle de séjour, où l'on peut prendre aussi ses repas. Délicieux lieux de détente : le bain à remous et le hamac.

Esta residencia se levanta sobre una colina y su diseño se integra perfectamente en el entorno rocoso y la vegetación silvestre. Como muestra de respeto por la naturaleza, se conservó un árbol que, ahora en el patio interior del edificio, tiñe el corazón de la casa de un intenso color rosa en la época de floración. El tejado está hecho de palmas cuidadosamente colocadas sobre una estructura de madera. Los lugares de estancia preferidos como, por ejemplo, un acogedor rincón que hace las veces de salón y comedor, se encuentran al aire libre, en la terraza cubierta. El jacuzzi y la hamaca son, sin duda, los mejores lugares para relajarse y disfrutar del ambiente.

Maui House

Architects: **Nick Malkovich and Arthur Erickson**
Location: **Maui, Hawaii, USA**
Photos: **© Ron Dahlquist**

This imposing house is perched on the edge of a low lava-stone cliff overlooking Makena beach on Maui's west coast. The house, which is surrounded by a lush tropical forest, almost appears to be sliding into the foamy Pacific below. Inasmuch as this section of the coast is protected by three reefs, the architect was able to place the house very close to the water. The house's extremely favourable location provides a commanding panoramic view up and down the coast through the glass facade. Viewed from the sea, the residence resembles a ship. This tapered swimming pool is directly adjacent to the deck and blends seamlessly into the dark blue of the sea in the distance.

Das imposante Haus thront in Makena am Rande einer niedrigen Klippe aus Lavagestein an der Westküste der Vulkaninsel Maui. Die Residenz ist umgeben von einem dichten Waldgebiet und scheint in der aufregenden Brandung des Pazifischen Ozeans fast unter zu gehen. Drei Riffe beschützen genau diesen Teil des Ufers und erlaubten so den Architekten das Haus so nah an das Wasser zu bauen. Die imposante Lage des Hauses ermöglicht eine beeindruckende Fernsicht auf die Küste durch die vordere Glasfassade. Vom Meer aus gesehen erscheint das Haus wie ein Schiff. Der spitz zulaufende Pool grenzt direkt an die Terrasse und geht nahtlos in das tiefe Blau des Hintergrundes über.

Cette maison majestueuse trône au bord d'une falaise de lave pétrifiée sur la côte ouest de l'île volcanique de Maui à Makena. La résidence, entourée d'une forêt épaisse, semble disparaître sous l'impressionnant déferlement des vagues du Pacifique. Seule cette partie du rivage est protégée par trois riffs permettant ainsi aux architectes de construire la maison si proche de l'eau. Grâce à cette situation imposante, on a, depuis la façade de verre antérieure, une vue grandiose sur la côte. Vu de la mer, la maison à l'allure d'un bateau. La pointe de la piscine adossée à la terrasse se jette directement dans le bleu profond de l'océan.

Esta impresionante casa está situada al borde de una formación rocosa de lava en la costa oeste de la isla volcánica de Maui, en Makena. La residencia, flanqueada por un cerrado bosque, parece ser devorada por las profundidades del mar debido al salvaje rompiente. Tres arrecifes protegen este tramo de costa, y ello permitió que el arquitecto pudiera construir la residencia próxima al agua. La arrebatadora situación de la casa posibilita una extensa e impresionante vista de la costa a través de la fachada de cristal. Visto desde el mar, el edificio parece un barco. La piscina rematada en punta limita la terraza y se extiende sin interrupción hasta el profundo azul del mar.

Volcano House

Architects: **De La Guardia Victoria Architects**
Location: **Hawaii, USA**
Photos: **© Jordi Miralles**

This imposing colonial style house is perched right at the edge of the Pacific. The glittering turquoise coloration of its striking swimming pool creates a bracing contrast with the deep blue of the sea. The rectangular pool is built around its own islet which is reached via two small bridges. The house itself blends marvellously into the volcanic surroundings both visually and in terms of the materials used. All floor and ground coverings are made of lava stone whose irregular shapes and striking red and yellow coloration are reminiscent of an erupting volcano.

Dieses mächtige Haus im Kolonialstil liegt direkt an der Küste des Pazifik. Der ausgefallene Swimming Pool bietet mit leuchtenden Türkisfarben einen erfrischenden Kontrast zum tiefblauen Ozean. Das Becken ist im Rechteck um eine eigene kleine Insel herum gebaut und auch über zwei Brücken erreichbar. Das Haus ist ausgezeichnet an seine vulkanreiche Umgebung angepasst, sowohl optisch als auch in Hinsicht auf die Materialien. Alle Böden vor und im Haus sind aus Lavagestein. Die roten und gelben Farben und Formen führen dazu, dass die Besucher das Gebäude als einen speienden Vulkan interpretieren.

Cette maison imposante, de style colonial, est située directement sur la côte Pacifique. La piscine, superbe d'originalité, aux tons de turquoise étincelants offre un contraste éclatant de fraîcheur face au bleu profond de l'océan. Le bassin rectangulaire, court autour d'un petit îlot et y est relié par deux ponts. La maison est parfaitement adaptée à l'environnement volcanique, tant sur le plan optique que pour le choix des matériaux. Les sols extérieurs et intérieurs sont en roches volcaniques. Les formes et couleurs rouges et jaunes de la demeure, créent l'illusion d'un volcan en éruption.

Esta poderosa casa de estilo colonial está situada justamente en la costa del Pacífico. La original piscina ofrece con su color turquesa brillante un llamativo contraste con el azul profundo del mar. Construida con forma rectangular alrededor de una pequeña isla, se accede a ella a través de dos puentes. La vivienda está perfectamente integrada en su entorno volcánico, tanto desde el punto de vista óptico como por los materiales escogidos. El suelo, dentro y fuera de la residencia, es de piedra volcánica. Sus tonalidades en rojo y amarillo y sus formas sugieren a los visitantes que interpreten la construcción como un volcán en erupción.

House on Hawaii

Architects: **By the residents**

Location: **Hawaii, USA**

Photos: **© Jordi Miralles**

This house is located in the middle of the vast Pacific Ocean on the island of Hawaii. As in most households in tropical regions, in this home life is mainly lived out of doors, and so here the roofed veranda is outfitted with a comfortable armchair, a table and a hammock. The house was built on low stilts in order to derive natural ventilation from the underlying air and to avoid having the entire mass of the structure rest on the ground, thus minimizing the environmental impact of the dwelling. The house's colorful decor with its exotic flowers and tropical fruits creates a cheery atmosphere.

Dieses Haus liegt inmitten des unendlichen Pazifik auf der Insel Hawaii. Wie bei den meisten Häusern in tropischen Regionen findet der Großteil des Lebens im Freien statt, so ist die überdachte Veranda mit einem gemütlichen Sessel, einem Tisch und einer Hängematte ausgestattet. Das Haus ist etwa einen Meter vom Erdboden aufgeständert, dies dient zur natürlichen Ventilation und gewährleistet zugleich, dass der Eingriff in die Natur minimal bleibt, da man den Boden nicht durch das gesamte Volumen des Hauses erdrückt. Die farbenfrohe Einrichtung samt den exotischen Blumen und tropischen Früchten sorgen für ein heiteres Ambiente.

Cette maison est située sur l'île d'Hawaii, au milieu de l'immensité de l'océan Pacifique. Comme dans la plupart des maisons tropicales, la majeure partie de la vie se déroule à l'air libre, la véranda est donc couverte et équipée d'un fauteuil confortable, d'une table et d'un hamac. La maison est surélevée de un mètre au-dessus du sol, pour permettre une ventilation naturelle, minimaliser en même temps l'empiètement sur la nature et ne pas écraser le sol sous le volume de la maison. L'aménagement aux couleurs vives conjugué aux fleurs exotiques et fruits tropicaux créent une ambiance d'allégresse.

Esta casa se sitúa en medio del vasto Pacífico, en la isla de Hawai. En las construcciones típicas de las regiones tropicales, la vida suele desarrollarse en el exterior; por ello, la veranda techada está dotada de un cómodo sillón, una mesa y una hamaca. El edificio se alza a 1 metro de altura, ello le confiere ventilación natural y, al mismo tiempo, hace que el impacto en la naturaleza sea mínimo, ya que el volumen de la construcción no descansa directamente sobre el suelo. La decoración colorista, las flores exóticas y las frutas tropicales crean un ambiente sereno y alegre.

Residence in Antigua

Interior Design: **Eric Ledoigt**

Location: **Antigua, Guatemala**

Photos: © **Reto Guntli**

Having sojourned for long periods in cities such as San Francisco and Paris, furtniture designer Eric Ledoigt found his personal idyll in Antigua. The cozy and rustic atmosphere of this venerable home reflects its owner's character, while it also showcases Ledoigt's designs as well as items he has collected during his travels in countries such as Japan, China, Thailand, Mexico and Morocco. The sunny inner courtyard at the center of the house contains countless plants and exotic flowers. Ledoigt, who is French, gladly takes his inspiration from nature. A stroll through the house's rooms and long corridors demonstrates the simplicity and sobriety on which his designs are based.

Nach langen Reisen und Aufenthalten in Städten wie San Francisco oder Paris hat der Möbeldesigner Eric Ledoigt sein individuelles Paradies in Antigua gefunden. Das alte Haus mit warmem und rustikalem Ambiente reflektiert den Charakter des Hausherren und präsentiert viele seiner persönlichen Arbeiten und auch Sammlerstücke aus unterschiedlichen Kulturen wie Japan, China, Thailand, Mexiko oder Marokko. Der sonnige Hof im Herzen des Hauses ist von unzähligen Pflanzen und exotischen Blumen bevölkert. Der Franzose lässt sich gerne durch die Natur inspirieren, und ein Rundgang durch die langen Flure und Räume des Hauses gleicht einem Lehrpfad über die Schlichtheit seiner Entwürfe.

Après de longs voyages et séjours dans des villes telles que San Francisco ou Paris Eric Ledoigt, designer de mobilier, a trouvé son petit coin de paradis à Antigua. La personnalité du maître des lieux se reflète dans cette maison ancienne à l'ambiance chaude et rustique. Nombre de ses œuvres personnelles et pièces de collection originaires du Japon, Chine, Thaïlande, Mexique ou Maroc, y sont exposées. Au cœur de la maison, la cour ensoleillée est agrémentée de mille et une plantes et fleurs exotiques. Ce designer français s'inspire volontiers de la nature. Flâner dans les longs couloirs et les pièces de la maison, est un véritable circuit éducatif à la découverte de ses créations aux formes épurées.

Después de largos viajes y estancias en ciudades como San Francisco o París, el diseñador de muebles Eric Ledoigt encontró su paraíso particular en Antigua. La vieja casa de ambiente cálido y rústico refleja el carácter de su propietario y presenta numerosos trabajos personales junto a piezas de colección de diferentes culturas como la japonesa, china, tailandesa, mexicana o marroquí. El soleado patio situado en el corazón del edificio está cubierto de innumerables plantas y exóticas flores. A Ledoigt le gusta inspirarse en la naturaleza; el recorrido por los largos pasillos y estancias de la casa nos da muestras de la sencillez y sobriedad en que se basan sus diseños.

House of the Orchids

Architect: **Chávez**

Interior Design: **Anna Isabel Carrera and Mario Montes**

Location: **Antigua, Guatemala**

Photos: **© Reto Guntli**

This majestic home is in Antigua, Guatemala, a city located in a volcanic area. An exotic garden rings the old wall of the house, which was once part of a convent. In 1988 the owners hired architect Chávez to create a design for what was then a dilapidated ruin. In creating the decor, Anna Isabel Carrera and Mario Montes went to great lengths to retain the atmosphere of the original building. The large windows and doors that were added all open onto the house's richly colored inner courtyard with its numerous fountains. The dining room is graced by an elegant chandelier, while a statue of a golden archangel watches over the the fireplace.

Dieses majestätische Haus liegt im vulkanreichen Gebiet von Antigua in Guatemala und hat Geschichte. Ein exotischer Garten umgibt das alte Gemäuer, das einst Teil eines Nonnenklosters war. 1988 beauftragte eine Familie den Architekten Chávez mit der Umgestaltung der bis dahin verwahrlosten Ruine. Anna Isabel Carrera und Mario Montes kümmerten sich dann um die Inneneinrichtung, wobei sie das Ambiente des Gebäudes weitgehend beibehielten. Es wurden große Fenster und Türen eingesetzt, die sich alle zum bunten Innenhof mit seinen zahlreichen Brunnen öffnen. Das Esszimmer wird von einem eleganten Kronleuchter erhellt und ein goldener Erzengel beschützt den Kamin.

Cette maison majestueuse, au passé chargé d'histoire, est située dans la région volcanique d'Antigua, au Guatemala. Un jardin exotique entoure une ancienne muraille de cloître de nonnes. En 1988, une famille a engagé l'architecte Chávez pour restaurer cette ruine abandonnée. Anna Isabel Carrera et Mario Montes chargés de la décoration intérieure, ont respecté, en grande partie, l'ambiance de la demeure d'origine. De grandes portes et fenêtres, s'ouvrent sur une cour intérieure haute en couleurs, aux nombreuses fontaines. Un lustre élégant illumine la salle à manger pendant qu'un archange protecteur doré trône au-dessus de la cheminée.

Esta majestuosa casa, situada en la región volcánica de Antigua, en Guatemala, tiene historia. Un exótico jardín rodea los viejos muros que antaño formaban parte de un convento de monjas. En 1988, la familia encargó al arquitecto Chávez la reconstrucción de la hasta entonces abandonada ruina. Anna Isabel Carrera y Mario Montes se ocuparon de la decoración interior y decidieron conservar el ambiente del edificio original. De esta manera, insertaron ventanas y puertas de gran formato, todas ellas abiertas al colorido patio interior con numerosas fuentes. El comedor se ilumina gracias a una elegante araña; y un arcángel dorado custodia la chimenea.

Thai Style House

Interior Design: **By the residents**
Location: **Río Dulce, Guatemala**
Photos: **© Reto Guntli**

This Guatemalan beach house, which was inspired by Asian culture, is situated between the Rio Dulce and the Gulf of Mexico. Slatted openings in the gables allow the heat that accumulates inside the house to rise, while numerous fans mounted on the house's crossbeams provide fresh, cooling air in the open interior space. The striking, split-level pool blends in visually with the sea, while the veranda is kept comfortably cool and shady by a thicket of tropical vegetation planted around it. The beach is only a stone's throw away, and the hammocks suspended over the water from the dock make for a pleasant place to commune with the ocean's mysteries.

Dieses durch die asiatische Kultur inspirierte Strandhaus befindet sich in Guatemala zwischen dem Fluss Rio Dulce und dem Golf von Mexico. Lamellenartige Schlitze im Dachgiebel gewährleisten, dass die aufsteigende Hitze im Inneren des Hauses nach oben abströmt. Außerdem sorgen auch hier zahlreiche, an Holzstreben angebrachte Ventilatoren für frische Luft im offenen Raum. Der ausgefallene Pool auf zwei Ebenen geht optisch in das weite Meer über. Die Veranda wird reichlich vom umgebenden tropischen Grün beschattet. Nur ein paar Stufen weiter hinunter gelangt man zum Strand und von dort aus auf den Bootssteg, wo eine Hängematte über dem Wasser schaukelt.

Cette maison de plage, aux influences des cultures asiatiques, se situe au Guatémala directement entre le fleuve Rio Dulce et le Golf du Mexique. Grâce à des fentes en forme de lamelles dans la charpente du toit, la chaleur intérieure monte et s'échappe vers le haut. Des ventilateurs fixés sur des montants de bois, garantissent également un apport d'air frais dans la pièce ouverte. Imposante par sa superbe, la piscine implantée sur deux niveaux donne l'illusion de se fondre à la mer. La véranda est ombragée à souhait par la verdure tropicale environnante. Quelques marches, en contrebas, suffisent pour atteindre la plage et un ponton d'où se balance un hamac, au-dessus de la mer.

Esta casa de playa de inspiración asiática se encuentra, sin embargo, en Guatemala, entre las aguas de Río Dulce y el Golfo de México. Las hendiduras laminadas en el aguilón del tejado se encargan de que el calor del interior del edificio se pierda por la parte superior. Además, los numerosos ventiladores aplicados en las vigas de madera garantizan aire frío a la estancia diáfana. La original piscina de dos niveles conduce la mirada hasta el ancho mar. Una veranda se cobija a la sombra de la abundante vegetación tropical. Unos escalones más abajo está la playa y, desde allí, al embarcadero donde una hamaca se bambolea sobre el mar.

91

House in Kingston

Architect: **David Chong**
Location: **Kingston, Jamaica**
Photos: © **Jaquiann Lawton, Compass Workshop**

This single family dwelling in Jamaica harmonizes optimally with the island's climate. Architect David Chong and his colleague Odell Williams constructed a house that is enclosed almost entirely by wooden slats which keep the hot sun out while allowing cooling air to waft through the house. Adjustable and rotatable doors and windows allow for the regulation of natural ventilation in accordance with wind direction and velocity. The house is equipped with natural air conditioning from below as well in that it is built on stilts.

Dieses Einfamilienhaus auf Jamaika ist vollkommen den klimatischen Bedingungen der Insel angepasst. Der Architekt David Chong baute gemeinsam mit seinem Kollegen Odell Williams ein Haus, das fast ausschließlich mit Lamellen aus Holz verschlossen ist. Sie hindern die Sonne daran, in das Haus einzudringen, während die Luft ungestört hindurchströmen kann. Die verstellbaren und drehbaren Türen und Fenster regulieren den Luftzug, je nachdem aus welcher Richtung und wie stark der Wind bläst. Sogar unter dem Haus erfolgt die Belüftung auf natürliche Weise, da das Haus auf Stelzen gebaut ist.

Cette maison individuelle en Jamaïque est entièrement adaptée aux conditions climatiques de l'île. En collaboration avec son collègue Odell Williams, l'architecte David Chong a construit une maison quasi entièrement fermée par des lamelles en bois. Empêchant le soleil de rentrer, elles permettent pourtant à l'air de circuler librement. Les portes et fenêtres mobiles et pivotantes règlent le courant d'air selon la direction et l'intensité du vent. Même sous la maison, l'aération est naturelle car la maison est construite sur pilotis.

Esta casa unifamiliar en Jamaica está totalmente adaptada a las condiciones climáticas de la isla. El arquitecto David Chong construyó, en colaboración con su colega Odell Williams, un edificio casi completamente cubierto de láminas de madera. De esta manera, se impide que el sol penetre en la vivienda y que el aire pueda circular sin problemas. Las puertas y ventanas corredizas y giratorias regulan la corriente según la dirección e intensidad del viento. La casa tiene incluso ventilación inferior natural, ya que está construida sobre pilotes.

Palmtree House

Architect: **Bill Cox**

Location: **Dominican Republic**

Photos: **© Pere Planells**

This house is located in Casa de Campo, a tony section of the village of La Romana, Dominican Republic. The nature of the ground necessitated building the house on three foot-high stilts, a common practice in the Dominican Republic. This horseshoe-shaped abode is made completely of wood with a swimming pool at its center. This also preserves the privacy of the pool area, from which there is a clear view of the Caribbean across an immaculately landscaped palm garden; a terrace surrounded by lush tropical vegetation affords a similar panorama. Residents have a breathtaking view from behind the house's all-glass facade, and lanterns scattered throughout the yard create a romantic atmosphere.

Dieses Haus steht in Casa de Campo, einer sehr luxuriösen Gegend des Dorfes La Romana in der Dominikanischen Republik. Es ist aufgrund der Bodenbeschaffenheit einen Meter vom Erdboden abgehoben, eine gängige Bauweise auf der Insel. Komplett aus Holz errichtet, ist es in U-Form um den Swimming Pool gebaut. Dadurch ist der Pool gut geschützt, und man kann vom Liegestuhl aus durch den gepflegten Palmengarten auf die Karibik blicken, wie auch von der von üppigen Pflanzen umgebenen Terrasse aus. Die Fassade ist rund herum aus Glas und gewährt auch vom Inneren eine atemberaubende Aussicht. Windlichter im gesamten Garten schaffen eine romantische Atmosphäre.

Cette maison se trouve à Casa de Campo, un quartier très luxueux du village La Romana de la République Dominicaine. Dû à la nature du terrain, la maison est surélevée d'un mètre par rapport au sol, une méthode de construction courante sur l'île. Grâce à sa disposition en U, la maison entièrement faite en bois entoure la piscine ainsi bien protégée. De la chaise longue, le regard peut flâner vers les Caraïbes du jardin de palmiers ou de la terrasse entourée de plantes exubérantes. La façade est entièrement en verre et permet même de l'intérieur une vue époustouflante. Des photophores éparpillés dans tout le jardin créent une atmosphère romantique.

Esta residencia está situada en Casa de Campo, una zona de lujo del pueblo La Romana, en la República Dominicana. Para protegerse de la humedad del suelo, esta casa de madera presenta la típica construcción de la isla, levantada a 1 metro de la superficie. La planta en forma de U rodea la piscina. Así, al tiempo que esta queda protegida, se puede contemplar el Caribe desde las tumbonas a través de un cuidado paisaje de palmeras o desde la terraza cubierta de exuberante vegetación. La fachada, totalmente de cristal, permite asimismo gozar de impresionantes vistas desde el interior. Las antorchas distribuidas por todo el jardín crean una romántica atmósfera.

House at Punta Cana

Architect: **Rina López**

Interior Design: **Haydée Rainieri and Oscar de la Renta**

Location: **Punta Cana, Dominican Republic**

Photos: © **Ricardo Labougle / Naty Abascal**

Haydée and Franck Rainieri are the owners of this attractive home which is located right on a picturesque Caribbean beach. The couple are also the founders of the magnificent Punta Cana Resort to which luminaries such as Julio Iglesias, Oscar de la Renta and Bill Clinton are drawn by the privacy and tranquility it offers. Haydée Rainieri and Oscar de la Renta collaborated on the interior design of the house whose decorative objects and wood furniture from Thailand and Chinese art lend the house a great deal of charm.

Haydée und Franck Rainieri sind die Besitzer dieser ansehnlichen Residenz direkt an einem malerischen Karibikstrand. Das Ehepaar hat einst gemeinsam das Tourismus-Imperium „Punta Cana Resort" gegründet, wo unter anderen Julio Iglesias, Oscar de la Renta und der ehemalige Präsident Clinton Ruhe suchten und die private Atmosphäre dieses Ortes genossen. Haydée Rainieri hat gemeinsam mit ihrem Kollegen Oscar de la Renta das Haus eingerichtet. Holzmöbel und Einrichtungsgegenstände aus Thailand und chinesische Kunst verleihen dem Haus seinen besonderen Charme.

Haydée et Franck Rainieri sont les propriétaires de cette jolie résidence située directement sur une plage pittoresque des Caraïbes. Le couple a fondé autrefois l'empire touristique « Punta Cana Resort », où, parmi d'autres, Julio Iglesias, Oscar de la Renta et l'ex-président Clinton ont cherché le repos et aussi pu jouir de l'atmosphère intime de cet endroit. Haydée Rainieri et son collègue Oscar de la Renta ont réalisé, ensemble, l'aménagement intérieur de cette résidence. Mobiliers en bois, éléments de décoration de Thaïlande et touches de art chinoise, confèrent à cette maison son charme particulier.

Haydée y Franck Rainieri son los propietarios de esta espectacular residencia situada en primera línea de una playa del pintoresco Caribe. El matrimonio fundó hace años el imperio turístico de Punta Cana Resort, donde buscan tranquilidad y disfrutan de la privacidad del lugar Julio Iglesias, Oscar de la Renta y el ex presidente Clinton, entre otros. Haydée Rainieri decoró la casa en colaboración con su amigo Oscar de la Renta. Muebles de madera, objetos decorativos de Tailandia y arte chino dan a la casa un particular encanto.

House at Punta Cana

Architect: **Oscar Imbert**
Location: **Punta Cana, Dominican Republic**
Photos: **© Ricardo Labougle / Naty Abascal**

Oscar Imbert, who designed the Punta Cana airport, also created this unique home. It is ensconced deep in the jungle and virtually the entire structure opens out onto the natural environment. The house is built exclusively from indigenous materials, which creates an authentic and pleasing synergy with its lush and unspoiled surroundings. The use of guayacan wood—one of the hardest and most durable tropical woods available—and the house's traditional architecture make the building far more resistant to hurricanes compared with modern structures. This 50-foot high, three-story house has five rooms and five bathrooms all of which open onto a central inner courtyard.

Oscar Imbert ist der Architekt des Flughafens von Punta Cana und hat unter anderem auch dieses einzigartige Haus inmitten des Dschungels entworfen, das sich fast komplett der Natur öffnet. Es wurden ausschließlich Baumaterialien aus der Region verwendet – dieses Haus geht wirklich eine Symbiose mit seiner Umgebung ein. Guayacan-Holz ist eines der härtesten und widerstandsfähigsten tropischen Hölzer. Dieses Material macht das Gebäude gemeinsam mit der ursprünglichen und traditionellen Bauweise weitaus widerstandsfähiger gegen Hurrikane als modernere Bauten. Das Haus besteht aus drei Stockwerken mit einer Gesamthöhe von 15 Metern. Es hat fünf Zimmer und fünf Badezimmer, die sich alle auf einen zentralen Innenhof hin öffnen.

Oscar Imbert est l'architecte de l'aéroport de Punta Cana. Il a aussi conçu, entre autres, cette maison exceptionnelle au milieu de la jungle, presque entièrement ouverte sur la nature. Pour cela, il n'a utilisé que des matériaux de construction issus de la région – cette maison est en véritable symbiose avec l'environnement. Le bois de Guayacan est un des bois tropicaux les plus durs et résistants. Ce matériau, allié à la conception de construction traditionnelle et originelle, rend cette maison bien plus résistante aux cyclones que les bâtiments modernes. Elle fait 15 mètres de haut, s'étend sur trois étages et dispose de cinq pièces et cinq salles de bains, toutes ouvertes sur la cour centrale.

Oscar Imbert es el arquitecto del aeropuerto de Punta Cana y responsable, entre otros proyectos, de esta particular casa en medio de la selva, que casi se abre en su totalidad a la naturaleza. Solamente se utilizaron materiales locales, por lo que el edificio se alza en verdadera simbiosis con el entorno. El guayacán es una de las maderas tropicales más duras y resistentes. Este material y la forma de construcción tradicional aseguran que la vivienda sea mucho más resistente a los huracanes que las estructuras modernas. La casa está compuesta de tres pisos con una altura total de 15 metros. Tiene cinco dormitorios y cinco cuartos de baño, abiertos todos ellos a un patio interior central.

House in San Juan

Interior Design: **Joanne Romanance**
Location: **Puerto Rico**
Photos: © **Pere Planells**

This renovated two-floor apartment with terrace is located in the heart of the colonial old town of San Juan, Puerto Rico. The apartment's owner, Joanne Romanance, is an artist and interior decorator whose sense of contemporary style is laced with a love for Mexico borne of a year-long soujourn south of the border. Romanance has decked her walls with crafts of diverse provenance, brightly colored wall murals and numerous paintings, while a flower motifed canvas rug that she created adorns her bedroom floor. In the bathroom the sink and mirror are deftly camouflaged behind tropical decorations and plants.

Das Apartment, eine renovierte zweistöckige Wohnung mit Terrasse, liegt im Zentrum des Kolonialviertels San Juan in Puerto Rico. Die Bewohnerin, Joanne Romanance, ist Künstlerin und Dekorateurin. Ihren modernen Stil mit mexikanischem Einfluss hat sie von einem jahrelangen Aufenthalt in Mexico mitgebracht. Neben Kunsthandwerk unterschiedlicher Art, farbenfrohen Wandbemalungen und den vielen Bildern hat die Künstlerin auch den auf Leinwand gemalten Teppich selbst geschaffen, der mit seinen blumigen Mustern das Schlafzimmer schmückt. Im Badezimmer sind Waschbecken und Spiegel hinter der tropischen Dekoration und den Pflanzen gut getarnt.

L'appartement, un logement de deux étages entièrement rénové, avec terrasse, est situé au cœur du quartier colonial de San Juan à Puerto Rico. Joanne Romanance, artiste et décoratrice y réside. Son style est moderne, influencé par le Mexique où elle a vécu de nombreuses années. A côté d'œuvres artisanales de différentes sortes, de peintures murales aux couleurs gaies, et de nombreux tableaux, l'artiste a créé le tapis peint sur toile aux motifs de fleurs qui décore la chambre à coucher. Dans la salle de bains, lavabo et miroir sont bien cachés derrière la décoration tropicale et les plantes.

Este apartamento, una vivienda de dos pisos con terraza recientemente reformada, está situado en el centro del barrio colonial de San Juan de Puerto Rico. La propietaria, Joanne Romanance, es artista y decoradora. Su moderno estilo, con clara influencia mexicana, se debe a su estancia en ese país durante largos años. Además de obras de artesanía de todo tipo, coloristas y alegres pinturas murales y muchos cuadros, la propia artista creó una alfombra pintada en lienzo, que con sus floridos motivos decora el dormitorio. En el baño, el lavabo y el espejo pasan desapercibidos a causa de la decoración tropical y las plantas.

House in Puerto Rico

Interior Design: **Luis Casañas**
Location: **El Condado, Puerto Rico**
Photos: © **Pere Planells**

This contemporary and remodelled early twentieth century home in the El Condado district, Puerto Rico is primarily made of wood and is built on approximately three foot-high stilts. This is a common practice in tropical climes that is designed to keep dampness out of the house and at the same time provide natural ventilation. The house is built to a square ground plan around an inner square courtyard which is a lovely place for the resident, an artist, to relax: here he is outside in the fresh air but is still sheltered in the center of the surrounding structure. This type of architecture brings nature inside while at the same time lightening the ambience of this rather enclosed design.

Dieses modern renovierte Haus im Viertel El Condado von Puerto Rico aus den Anfängen des 20. Jahrhunderts besteht überwiegend aus Holz und ist etwa einen Meter vom Erdboden abgehoben auf Stelzen gebaut. Diese in tropischen Klimazonen gängige Bauweise dient dazu, das Haus vor Feuchtigkeit zu schützen und eine natürliche Ventilation zu erzeugen. Das Haus hat einen quadratischen Grundriss und ist um einen viereckigen Innenhof herum gebaut. Er ist ein herrlicher Platz zum Entspannen für den Eigentümer, einen Künstler, da er zwar unter freiem Himmel, aber gut geschützt im Herzen des Hauses liegt. Durch diese Bauweise wird ein Stück Natur ins Haus mit einbezogen und der geschlossene Entwurf etwas aufgelockert.

Cette maison modernisée du début des années vingt, située dans le quartier d'El Condado de Puerto Rico et conçue presque entièrement en bois, est construite près d'un mètre au-dessus du sol. Cette méthode courante dans les zones climatiques tropicales garantit une protection contre l'humidité et une ventilation naturelle. La maison dotée d'un plan d'ensemble quadrangulaire est structurée autour d'un patio carré. Grâce à cet endroit superbe, à ciel ouvert mais parfaitement protégé au cœur de la maison, son propriétaire, un artiste, peut s'y détendre à loisir. Cette forme de construction intègre un pan de nature dans la maison et aère d'une certaine façon le plan fermé.

Esta residencia recientemente modernizada del barrio de El Condado, en Puerto Rico, fue construida en la década de los veinte. Elaborada casi en su totalidad en madera, se erige a una altura de 1 metro sobre el suelo. Este tipo de edificación, muy usual en zonas de clima tropical, protege de la humedad y crea una ventilación natural. La vivienda, de planta cuadrangular, se extiende alrededor de un patio de idéntica forma. Para su propietario, artista de profesión, este es un lugar perfecto para el descanso: al aire libre pero protegido por el corazón de la casa, incorpora la naturaleza a la vivienda y suaviza la concepción cerrada de la construcción.

Stickland Villa

Architects: **acla:works**
Location: **Trinidad Tobago**
Photos: **© Brian Lewis**

This Caribbean vacation home is Billy and Lisa Stickland's refuge from the hurlyburly of everyday life. Here this Irish couple can relax and enjoy the humid tropical climate as they gaze meditatively into the distance from their veranda or from their swimming pool deck. Stickland Villa is truly a dream house, and while it is of course air-conditioned, the master bedroom deck is outfitted with fans that provide additional air circulation. The floors of the house are made of hand-decorated glazed tiles and all of the doors, windows and closets have been executed in wood. The interior decor was realized in indigenously produced materials only.

Dieses Ferienhaus in der Karibik ist für die Besitzer Billy und Lisa Stickland aus Irland eine Zuflucht vor dem Alltagsstress. Hier können sie das tropisch feuchte Klima in sich aufnehmen und auf der Veranda oder am Swimming Pool den Geist in die Ferne schweifen lassen. Dieses Haus erfüllt höchste Ansprüche und verfügt selbstverständlich auch über eine Klimaanlage. Abgesehen davon sind an der Decke des Schlafzimmers Ventilatoren angebracht, die für zusätzliche Luftzirkulation sorgen. Die Böden bestehen aus handgemalten, glasierten Tonkacheln und alle Türen, Fenster und Schränke sind aus Holz. Für die Errichtung des gesamten Hauses wurden nur vor Ort hergestellte Baustoffe verwendet.

Cette maison de vacances, située au Caraïbes, permet à ses propriétaires irlandais, Billy et Lisa Stickland, de s'évader de la vie quotidienne. Là, ils peuvent s'imprégner du climat tropical humide et, sur la véranda ou au bord de la piscine, laisser leur esprit vagabonder au loin. Cette maison, répondant à de hauts critères d'exigences, est bien sur climatisée. De surcroît, des ventilateurs sont fixés au plafond de la chambre à coucher pour un apport d'air supplémentaire. Les sols sont recouverts de carrelage en terre cuite émaillée et peinte à la main ; toutes les portes, fenêtres et armoires sont en bois. Les matériaux utilisés pour la construction de la maison, sont essentiellement produits localement.

Esta casa de vacaciones, situada en el Caribe, es para sus propietarios irlandeses, Billy y Lisa Stickland, un refugio del estrés cotidiano. Aquí pueden disfrutar del clima tropical y, acomodados en la veranda o en la piscina, dejar que su espíritu vague libre. Esta casa responde a las necesidades más exigentes y, por supuesto, tiene aire acondicionado. Además, el dormitorio presenta ventiladores de techo que crean, adicionalmente, corrientes de aire. El suelo está recubierto de baldosas de barro cocido, esmaltadas y pintadas a mano, y todas las puertas, ventanas y armarios son de madera. Se utilizaron exclusivamente materiales locales para la construcción del edificio.

Villa Petrus

Architects: **acla:works**
Location: **Trinidad Tobago**
Interior Designers: **Design Studios**
Photos: **© Andy Birchall**

Villa Petrus is an opulent Tobagan house on two acres of land with a 65-foot swimming pool. As the house is situated on a hill, it benefits from ample natural ventilation and affords Gary Stephens and his wife a fantastic panoramic view of the Caribbean. This impressive and luxurious home offers its owners every conceivable modern comfort and convenience. The house has seven bedrooms with air-condition and six bathrooms. A separate apartment has a kitchen and living room. Each room in the house has its own color, and the rooms can accommodate up to 14 people at a time.

Die Villa Petrus ist ein luxuriöses Haus in Tobago auf zwei Morgen Land mit einem Swimming Pool von 20 m Länge. Durch die Lage auf den Hügeln können die natürlichen Luftströmungen genutzt werden. Außerdem bietet sie Gary Stephens und seiner Frau eine herrliche Aussicht auf das Karibische Meer. Dieser Wohnsitz strahlt Erhabenheit und Reichtum aus und bietet jeden Komfort des modernen Lebens. Es gibt sieben Schlafzimmer mit Klimaanlage und sechs Badezimmer. Außerdem befindet sich im Anbau eine unabhängige Suite mit separater Küche und Wohnzimmer. Jeder Raum des Ensembles hat eine andere Farbe. Die großzügigen Zimmer können insgesamt bis zu 14 Personen beherbergen.

La Villa Petrus est une maison luxueuse à Tobago, construite sur deux arpents de terre, avec une piscine de 20 m de long. Située sur la colline, elle jouit d'une ventilation naturelle et offre à ses occupants, Gary Stephens et son épouse une vue extraordinaire sur la mer des Caraïbes. Noblesse et richesse émanent de cette résidence qui offre tout le confort de la vie moderne. Il y a sept chambres climatisées et six salles de bains. A cela s'ajoute une annexe avec une suite indépendante dotée d'une cuisine séparée et d'un salon. Chaque pièce de cet ensemble a sa propre couleur. Les chambres, spacieuses, peuvent héberger jusqu'à 14 personnes.

Villa Petrus es una lujosa casa de Tobago, que ocupa dos fanegas de tierra y posee una piscina de 20 metros de largo. Gracias a su situación privilegiada, sobre las colinas, disfruta de corrientes naturales de aire. Además, ofrece a los propietarios, Gary Stephens y su mujer, estupendas vistas sobre el mar Caribe. Esta residencia irradia solemnidad y opulencia, y ofrece todas las comodidades de la vida moderna. Tiene siete dormitorios con aire acondicionado y seis cuartos de baño. Actualmente, se está construyendo además una suite independiente con cocina y sala de estar propias. Cada habitación del conjunto está pintada en un color diferente. Las generosas estancias pueden acoger hasta 14 personas.

House in Colombia

Architect: **Simon Vélez**

Location: **Colombia**

Photos: **© Undine Pröhl**

This Colombian house was built on a 107,000 square foot piece of property that is traversed by two streams. One of them runs right in front of the entrance to the house, prompting the architect to construct a lovely footbridge directly facing the staircase leading up to the house, which is on a slight rise and consists of three wings. One contains the living areas, a second the kitchen and dining area and the third a partially covered bathroom for the pool. The house is mainly made of bamboo, which is one of the least expensive building materials in Colombia. The stone floors help keep the house cool.

Dieses Haus steht in Kolumbien auf einem weitläufigen Grundstück von 10.000 m². Zwei kleine Bäche kreuzen das Gelände, einer davon direkt vor dem Eingang, sodass der Architekt eine charmante Holzbrücke vor die Treppenstufen gebaut hat. Das Haus steht auf einer leichten Anhöhe und besteht aus drei Pavillons. Einer davon beherbergt den Wohnbereich, ein Weiterer die Küche und das Esszimmer und der Dritte das halb offene Badezimmer für den Pool. Das Haus besteht hauptsächlich aus Bambus, eines der günstigsten Baumaterialien in Kolumbien. Die Steinböden haben einen kühlenden Effekt.

Cette maison se trouve en Colombie sur un vaste terrain de 10.000 m². Traversé par deux petits ruisseaux dont un directement devant l'entrée, l'architecte a fait construire un ravissant pont en bois devant les escaliers. La maison située sur une petite colline est composée de trois pavillons. L'un abrite le séjour, l'autre, la cuisine et la salle à manger et le troisième, la salle de bains à moitié ouverte pour la piscine. La maison est conçue essentiellement de bambou, l'un des matériaux de construction les plus avantageux en Colombie. Les sols en pierres ont un effet rafraîchissant.

Esta casa colombiana se levanta sobre una enorme finca de 10.000 m². De los dos arroyos que cruzan el terreno, uno fluye directamente por delante de la entrada. Esto motivó al arquitecto la construcción de un encantador puente frente a los escalones de acceso. El edificio se alza sobre una loma y se compone de tres pabellones. El primero acoge las zonas de estancia; el segundo, la cocina y el comedor, y el tercero, el cuarto de baño semiabierto para la piscina. La casa está edificada principalmente con bambú, un material de construcción que en Colombia resulta muy económico. Los suelos de piedra conservan el ambiente fresco en la vivienda.

House of the Mirrors

Architects: **José María Rodríguez and Ivonne Valencia**
Collaboration: **María Isabel López and Oscar Montalegre**
Location: **Anapoima, Colombia**
Photos: **© Jorge Gamboa**

The central architectural element of this house is a series of inner courtyards with pools. The various areas are connected by small wooden bridges and each has its own distinctive character. The patio pools act as mirrors that reflect the house's architecture and make the trees look like undulating islands while at the same they keep the ambient environment cool. The star of the show here is the swimming pool: it is right next to one side of the living room, which is unenclosed and opens out in several directions. The front of the living room gives onto the terrace and a garden. The smoothly angled forms of this house are echoed by the water that is such an integral part of it.

Eine Struktur aus mehreren Innenhöfen mit Wasserbecken wurde als zentrales Element dieses Hauses entworfen, bei dem jeder Bereich unterschiedlich aussieht. Der Rundgang wird durch kleine Brücken aus Holz gegliedert. Diese Wasserpatios wirken wie Spiegel, welche die Architektur reflektieren, die Bäume optisch wie Inseln schwimmen lassen und gleichzeitig kühlen. Der Pool ist der Hauptdarsteller dieser Anlage und grenzt direkt an eine Seite des zu mehreren Richtungen geöffneten Wohnzimmers. Nach vorne hinaus führt das Wohnzimmer auf die Terrasse und den Garten. Die glatten und rechtwinkligen Formen dieses Hauses werden durch das Wasser unterstrichen.

Cette maison est conçue autour d'un élément central : une structure composée de plusieurs cours intérieures agrémentées de bassins d'eau. Chaque partie de cette espace habité est différente et on en fait le tour grâce à une série de petits ponts de bois. Ces patios d'eau qui rafraîchissent l'atmosphère, sont comme des miroirs où l'architecture se reflète et où les arbres semblent nager, tels des îles. Dans cet ensemble, la piscine a le rôle principal. Elle jouxte directement un pan du séjour ouvert sur plusieurs côtés. Devant, le séjour s'ouvre sur la terrasse et le jardin. L'eau souligne les formes lisses et angulaires de cette maison.

Una estructura de varios patios interiores y estanques de agua es el elemento central de esta casa, en la que cada zona tiene una atmósfera diferente. El paseo por este complejo se lleva a cabo a través de una serie de puentes de madera. Los patios llenos de agua son como espejos que reflejan la arquitectura, hacen nadar a los árboles a modo de islas y refrescan el ambiente. La piscina es la protagonista de este complejo y limita directamente con uno de los lados de la sala de estar, abierta en varias direcciones. Por su parte delantera, el salón conduce a la terraza y al jardín. El agua por doquier subraya las formas rectas y angulosas de la casa.

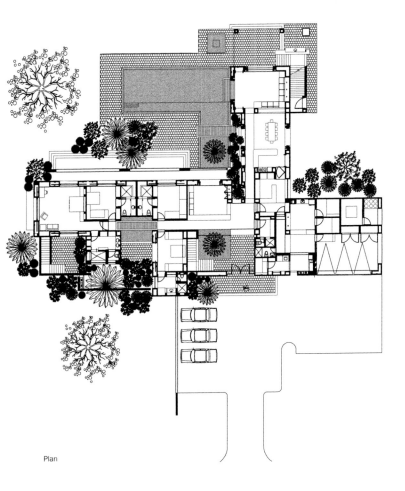

Plan

Open House

Architect: **José Maria Rodríguez and Ivonne Valencia**

Location: **Barichara, Colombia**

Photos: **© Jorge Gamboa**

This house is located in Bichara, a typical colonial-era village in Colombia, with a long and noble tradition of tobacco and hemp growing. Houses in this region are generally made of clay brick with crudely plastered walls. This house stands on the site of a square where there used to be the drying place and the original structures on this square have been retained. The house consists of a large, roofed living area devoid of doors or enclosed walls, and has two separate bedrooms. The bathroom is located in a smaller room where farmers once stored their tools and materials.

Das Haus befindet sich in Bichara, einem der repräsentativsten Kolonialdörfer Kolumbiens mit einer bedeutenden und langjährigen Tradition des Tabak- und Sisalanbaus. Bei Häusern in dieser Region werden üblicherweise die Mauern aus Lehmziegeln gebaut und die Wände grob verputzt. Bei dem Bau wurde die Originalstruktur eines Trockenplatzes beibehalten – er besteht aus einem großen, überdachten Wohnbereich ohne geschlossene Wände oder Türen und zwei abgetrennten Schlafzimmern. In einem kleineren Raum, der einst zur Lagerung von Materialien und Werkzeugen der Bauern diente, befindet sich heute das Badezimmer.

La maison est située à Bichara, un des villages coloniaux le plus représentatif de Colombie avec une longue tradition de plantation de tabac et de chanvre de sisal. Les murailles des maisons de cette région sont généralement construites en briques de terre glaise dont les murs sont grossièrement crépis. La structure originelle de l'ancien séchoir, préservée lors de la construction, se compose d'une grande pièce à vivre, abritée sous un toit, dépourvue de murs fermés ou de portes, avec deux chambres à coucher séparées. Une petite pièce, jadis un d'entrepôt de matériel et d'outil des paysans, accueille aujourd'hui la salle de bains.

Esta casa se encuentra en Bichara, uno de los pueblos coloniales más representativos de Colombia, con una significativa y larga tradición del cultivo de tabaco y cáñamo de pita. Las casas de esta región suelen tener muros de adobe y paredes toscamente revocadas. En la construcción de esta residencia se respetó la estructura original del antiguo secadero; la vivienda está compuesta de una estancia amplia y techada sin puertas ni tabiques, y dos dormitorios separados. Una pequeña habitación, que antaño servía para guardar los materiales y las herramientas de los campesinos, acoge en la actualidad el cuarto de baño.

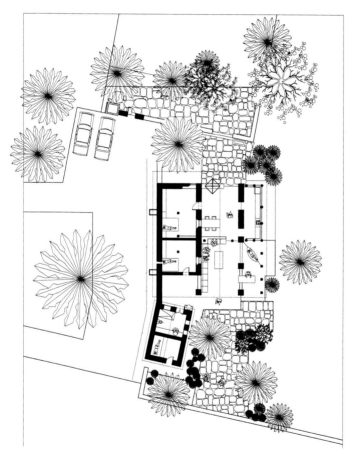

Plan

Rock Island

Architect: **Alberto Burckhardt**

Location: **Rosario Islands, Colombia**

Photos: © **Silvia Patiño**

Built on a wispy island consisting of two rocks, this house is part of Rosario archipelago nature preserve in Colombia. The island was uninhabited for many years and is thus completely overgrown. The challenge facing the architect was to create a contemporary home that would also harmonize with the Carribbean atmosphere, typified here by the wooden pergolas that filter the light and by the rattan banisters and wood decks that link the exterior and interior of the house. The main house, walkways and detached buildings are made of indigenous mecana and teak, which are extremely durable and high quality woods.

Dieses Projekt wurde auf einer winzigen Insel realisiert, die aus zwei Felsen besteht. Sie ist Teil des Naturschutzgebietes des Rosario-Archipels in Kolumbien. Die Insel war viele Jahre verwaist und ist daher völlig verwildert. Die Herausforderung des Architekten bestand darin, einen modernen Wohnsitz zu schaffen, der sich der karibischen Atmosphäre anpasst. Typische Beispiele hierfür sind die hölzernen Pergolen, die das Licht filtern, die Rattan-Geländer und Holzterrassen, die Innen- und Außenbereich verbinden. Für Haus, Pavillon und Stege wurden Mecana und Teak verwendet, einheimische Hölzer von hoher Qualität und Widerstandskraft.

C'est un projet réalisé sur une toute petite île, faite de deux rochers qui fait partie de la réserve naturelle de l'archipel Rosario en Colombie. Abandonnée pendant plusieurs années, l'île est à l'état sauvage complet. L'architecte a fait face au défi de réaliser une résidence moderne, adaptée à l'atmosphère des Caraïbes en utilisant des éléments typiques : pergolas en bois qui filtrent la lumière, balustrades de rotin et terrasses en bois, traits-d'union entre l'espace extérieur et intérieur. Maison, pavillon et pontons sont en mecana et bois de teck, bois locaux d'excellente qualité et très résistants.

Este proyecto se llevó a cabo en un minúsculo islote compuesto únicamente por dos rocas, parte integrante del parque natural del archipiélago de Rosario, en Colombia. La isla permaneció deshabitada durante años y, por lo tanto, se encontraba en estado salvaje. El reto para el arquitecto era la creación de una residencia moderna que se adaptase al ambiente caribeño. Para ello, los típicos recursos son las pérgolas de madera que filtran la luz, las superficies de rota y las terrazas de madera que unifican el espacio exterior e interior. Para la construcción de la casa, el cenador y el embarcadero se utilizaron mecana y teca, maderas autóctonas de gran calidad y resistencia.

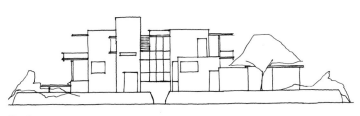

Elevation

Brasilian Dream

Interior Designer: **By the residents**
Location: **Praia Do Roso, Brazil**
Photos: **© Ricardo Labougle**

From this cozy little house perched on a hillside the people and fishing boats look like little dots of color in the sand of the lagoon. A curtain of lush vegetation in front of the house affords plenty of opportunity for dreamy contemplation of the endless blue expanse beyond. This exotic idyll of a home ensconced in the midst of intense green vegetation soothes the soul. The house's extremely basic decor radiates a powerful earthiness, a reflection of the joyful and harmonious atmosphere that has been created with minimal effort out of local materials. A wooden staircase leads up to the bedroom area where the hypnotic chittering of cicadas makes for pleasant dreams.

Dieses gemütliche Häuschen ist am Hang gelegen und von weitem wirken die Menschen und Fischerboote wie bunte Farbtupfer im Sand der Lagune. Hinter der saftigen Vegetation können die Gedanken im uferlosen Blau versinken. Hier herrscht exotische Idylle inmitten intensiven Grüns, die das Gemüt beruhigt. Das Heim ist mit einfachsten Mitteln eingerichtet und strahlt eine erstaunliche Natürlichkeit aus. Aus örtlichen Materialien wurde ohne viel Aufwand eine Atmosphäre voller Lebensfreude und Harmonie geschaffen. Über eine Holztreppe gelangt man in das Schlafquartier, wo hypnotisches Zirpen angenehme Träume verspricht.

Cette petite maison confortable est implantée sur la colline et vu de loin, les hommes et les bateaux de pécheurs paraissent être des touches multicolores sur le sable de la lagune. Au-delà de la végétation luxuriante, les pensées peuvent se perdre dans le bleu illimité. C'est le royaume de l'idylle exotique au milieu d'un vert intense qui apaise l'âme. La maison, construite avec des moyens très simples, dégage une ambiance naturelle surprenante. L'emploi de matériaux régionaux, peu coûteux, créé une atmosphère harmonieuse, remplie de joie de vivre. Un escalier de bois conduit aux chambres à coucher où le chant hypnotisant des cigales promet des rêves agréables.

Esta confortable casita está situada en una ladera y desde ella, las personas y los botes de los pescadores se ven como minúsculos puntos de color sobre la arena de la laguna. La mente se puede perder tras la suave vegetación en la inmensidad del azul de las aguas. En medio del verdor reina un exótico idilio que calma el espíritu. La casa está decorada con los medios más sencillos e irradia una impresionante naturalidad. Con ayuda de materiales autóctonos, se logró crear sin mucha suntuosidad un ambiente lleno de alegría y de armonía. Una escalera de madera nos conduce a la zona de los dormitorios donde el hipnótico canto de las chicharras promete agradables sueños.

213

Tropical Residence

Interior Design: **Viviane Sampaio**
Location: **Rio de Janeiro, Brazil**
Photos: © **Reto Guntli**

For decades now, antique dealer Viviane Sampaio has been scouring the planet for collector's items and antiques. Her grandparents emigrated to Rio de Janeiro following World War I and in the 1950s found a piece of property they wanted and built their dream house on it. Viviane's grandmother had the house painted lavender, a color that creates a cheery mood and whose glowing luminousness vies with the orchids. A bed ensconced on the patio in the deep cool shade of tropical plants is perfect for siestas in this soft pastel ambience. The wall above is decorated with antique Portuguese tiles. The chandelier in the master bedroom has particular sentimental value having been originally installed by Viviane's grandfather.

Die Antiquitätenhändlerin Viviane Sampaio reiste jahrzehntelang um die Welt, ständig auf der Suche nach Antiquitäten und Sammlerstücken. Ihre Großeltern kamen nach dem ersten Weltkrieg nach Rio, wo sie in den 1950er Jahren das Grundstück fanden und ihr Traumhaus bauten. Damals ließ es ihre Großmutter violett anstreichen, eine Farbe, die optimistisch stimmt und mit den Orchideen um die Wette leuchtet. Für die Siesta im rosigen Ambiente wartet auf der Terrasse ein Bett im Schatten der tropischen Blätter. Die Wand darüber ist mit antiken Kacheln aus Portugal geschmückt. Der Kronleuchter im Schlafzimmer ist ein Erinnerungsstück, Vivianes Großvater hat ihn gebaut.

L'antiquaire Viviane Sampaio a voyagé des décénnies autour du monde, toujours en quête d'antiquités et d'objets d'art. Après la Première Guerre Mondiale, ses grands-parents se sont installés à Rio, où ils ont trouvé dans les années 1950 le terrain pour y construire la maison de leur rêve. A l'époque, ce fut sa grand-mère qui la fit peindre en violet, une couleur qui rend optimiste et qui rivalise avec l'éclat des orchidées. Un lit attend à l'ombre des feuilles tropicales pour la sieste sur la terrasse dans une ambiance de vie en rose. Le mur au-dessus est paré de faïences antiques du Portugal. Dans la chambre à coucher, le lustre conçu par le grand-père de Viviane, est un souvenir personnel.

La anticuaria Viviane Sampaio se dedicó durante décadas a viajar por todo el mundo en busca de antigüedades y piezas de coleccionismo. Sus abuelos llegaron a Río de Janeiro después de la Primera Guerra Mundial, donde en la década de los cincuenta compraron un solar y edificaron la casa de sus sueños. La abuela de Viviane mandó pintar la construcción de violeta, un color optimista que rivaliza en luminosidad con las orquídeas. Una cama situada en la terraza, a la sombra de las plantas tropicales, se convierte en el ambiente ideal para disfrutar de una reconfortante siesta. La araña de cristal encierra un valor sentimental: instalada por el abuelo de Viviane, adorna la habitación principal.

Beach House

Architect: **Claudio Bernardes**
Location: **Rio de Janeiro, Brazil**
Photos: **© Reto Guntli**

In this house, architect Claudio Bernardes has blended his own style with the origins of Brazilian architecture and the crafts of indigenous Brazilian ethnic groups. The result is a highly original house which is made of various types of wood and bamboo and which eschews doors and windows in favor of a structure that is completely open to the external environment, making the house itself part of the breathtaking landscape in which it is set. A friend of the architect's, the artist Jorge dos Anjos, decorated the weight bearing wood pillars with indigenous ethnic motifs, while the richly colored decor creates a cheery atmosphere and harmonizes with the exotic plants in and around the house.

Der Architekt Claudio Bernardes hat beim Bau dieses Hauses die Ursprünge der brasilianischen Architektur und indianisches Kunsthandwerk mit seinem persönlichen Stil kombiniert. Das Ergebnis ist ein komplett mit verschiedenen Holzsorten und Bambus verkleidetes, höchst originelles Haus, das weder Türen noch Fenster hat, sondern sich völlig zur Natur öffnet. So wird es zu einem Teil der atemberaubenden Landschaft. Der Künstler Jorge dos Anjos, ein Freund des Architekten, verzierte die tragenden Holzpfeiler mit indianischen Mustern. Die farbenfrohe Dekoration provoziert gute Laune und harmoniert mit den exotischen Pflanzen im und um das Haus.

En concevant cette maison, l'architecte Claudio Bernardes a su marier les origines de l'architecture brésilienne et de l'artisanat indien à son style personnel. Il en résulte une maison fort originale, entièrement habillée en bois et bambous aux essences diverses, dépourvue de portes et fenêtres, complètement ouverte sur la nature. Elle devient alors partie intégrante du paysage époustouflant. L'artiste Jorge dos Anjos, ami de l'architecte, a orné les piliers porteurs en bois de motifs indiens. La décoration aux couleurs vives incitant à la bonne humeur est en harmonie avec les plantes exotiques de la maison et des alentours.

El arquitecto Claudio Bernardes combinó en la construcción de esta casa la arquitectura autóctona de Brasil y la artesanía indígena con su estilo personal. El resultado es una residencia extremadamente original, revestida con diferentes tipos de madera y con bambú, sin puertas ni ventanas, que se abre completamente a la naturaleza. De esta forma, se convierte en parte importante del impresionante paisaje. El artista Jorge dos Anjos, un amigo del arquitecto, recubrió los pilares de madera de motivos indígenas. La decoración invita al buen humor y armoniza con las plantas exóticas del interior y exterior de la vivienda.

House in Rio

Architect: **Janete Costa**

Location: **Rio de Janeiro, Brazil**

Photos: **© Reto Guntli**

The architect Janete Costa lives in this house which is located in a residential neighborhood above Avenida Niemeyer and alongside Leblon beach in Ipanema. Costa and her friend and colleague, the legendary landscape architect Roberto Burle Marx, worked together on designing and creating the garden of this artistic gem of a home. Costa owns an eclectic collection of traditional Brazilian folk art, Portuguese baroque statuettes and modern design objects. She also organizes large public art exhibitions and previews and is a great promoter of the art, artists and culture of northeastern Brazil.

Die Architektin Janete Costa lebt selbst in diesem Haus in einer Wohnsiedlung über der Avenida Niemeyer am Strand entlang von Leblon bei Ipanema. Gemeinsam mit ihrem Freund und Kollegen Roberto Burle Marx, eine Ikone der Landschaftsarchitektur, gestaltete sie den Garten ihres kunstvollen Hauses. Janete Costa besitzt eine eklektische Sammlung traditioneller Volkskunst aus Brasilien, portugiesischer Barockfiguren sowie moderner Designobjekte. Sie organisiert große Ausstellungen und Vernissagen und fördert insbesondere die Kultur und ihre Künstler aus dem Nordosten Brasiliens.

C'est la maison privée de l'architecte Janete Costa, située dans un quartier résidentiel de l'Avenida Niemeyer, sur la plage, le long de Leblon près d'Ipanema. L'architecte a aménagé le jardin de sa villa très artistique, en collaboration avec son collègue et ami Roberto Burle Marx, une référence dans le domaine de l'architecture paysagiste. Janete Costa possède une collection éclectique d'art populaire traditionnel du Brésil, de personnages baroques portugais et d'objets de design moderne. En organisant de grandes expositions et des vernissages, elle soutient tout particulièrement la culture et les artistes de la côte nord-est du Brésil.

La arquitecta Janete Costa vive en esta casa que ella misma construyó en un complejo residencial de la avenida Niemeyer, en la playa de Leblon de Ipanema. Con ayuda de su novio y colega, Roberto Burle Marx, un icono de la arquitectura paisajista, diseñó el jardín de la estilizada casa. Janete Costa posee una ecléctica colección de arte brasileño, imaginería del barroco portugués y modernos muebles de diseño. Suele organizar importantes exposiciones y eventos con los que pretende promocionar, sobre todo, la cultura y los artistas de la región más nororiental de Brasil.

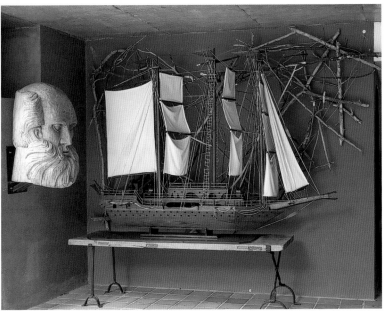

Bicalho Beach House

Architect: **Paulo Bicalho and Fernando Nunan**

Decoration: **Studio Due**

Location: **San Sebastian, Brazil**

Photos: © **Wagner Souza e Silva**

The tower at the architectonic center of this contemporary home accommodates both a staircase and a gravity flow water tank. The blue fiberglass on the exterior of the tower reflects the sun, thereby keeping the interior cool, while the attic space has been specially designed to provide natural ventilation. An L-shaped pool with a waterfall makes the yard a lovely place in which to relax. Sliding glass doors open onto the interconnected living room and kitchen, while a spiral staircase leads up to a deck which has a jacuzzi and a small sitting area with a view of soothing greenness. The bedrooms in the upper part of the house are accessed from this deck as well.

Die vertikale Hauptachse dieses modernen Hauses bildet ein Turm, der als Treppenaufgang und gleichzeitig als Wasserspeicher dient. Er ist von außen mit blauen Glasfasern beschichtet, die die Sonne reflektieren, und erzeugt somit einen thermischen Effekt. Unter dem Dach ist ein Hohlraum zur natürlichen Belüftung vorgesehen. Ein L-förmiger Pool mit Wasserfall erfrischt das Klima im Garten. Glasschiebetüren öffnen sich zu Wohnzimmer und Küche, die auch miteinander verbunden sind. Eine spiralförmige Treppe führt auf eine Terrasse, wo sich ein Whirlpool und eine kleine Sitzecke mit Blick ins Grüne befindet. Von hier aus gelangt man auch zu den Schlafzimmern im oberen Bereich.

L'axe principale et verticale de cette maison moderne est une tour servant en même de temps d'escalier et de réservoir d'eau. De dehors, elle est recouverte de fibres de verres bleues reflétant le soleil et créant ainsi un effet thermique. Sous le toit, un espace vide permet une ventilation naturelle. Une piscine en forme de L, dotée d'une cascade, rafraîchit le climat du jardin. Des baies vitrées coulissantes s'ouvrent sur le salon et la cuisine, eux-mêmes reliés entre eux. Un escalier hélicoïdal amène vers une autre terrasse abritant un jacuzzi et un petit coin pour s'asseoir avec vue sur la verdure. D'ici, on accède aux chambres à coucher situées à l'étage supérieur.

El eje vertical principal de esta moderna casa forma una torre que sirve tanto de escalera como de depósito de agua; recubierta exteriormente con fibra de cristal azul, refleja el sol y produce un efecto térmico. Bajo el tejado hay un espacio hueco diseñado especialmente para proporcionar ventilación natural. La piscina en forma de L con una cascada de agua conciben el jardín como un lugar agradable para el relax. Las puertas correderas de cristal se abren a la sala y a la cocina, que a su vez están comunicadas entre sí. Una escalera en forma de espiral conduce a una terraza con un jacuzzi y un pequeño rincón acondicionado para sentarse y contemplar la naturaleza. Desde aquí se accede a los dormitorios del piso superior.

House in Los Cabos

Architect: **Alan Faena**
Location: **Los Cabos, Uruguay**
Photos: **© Reto Guntli**

This house is notable for its spaciousness and elongated groundplan. A white wood veranda parallels the turquoise facade of a home whose decor is a celebration of color. A relatively large room containing areas for various activities forms the center of the dwelling. The dining room is adjacent to the livingroom which also contains a small office. Further behind a bed has been positioned directly facing an antique bathtub. Style, color and imagination have been elegantly blended, but traditional forms and materials have also been deployed to good effect.

Großzügige Dimensionen und eine weite horizontale Linienführung sind die Besonderheiten dieses Hauses. Eine weiße Holzveranda führt entlang der türkisenen Fassade in das Haus mit seiner farbenfrohen Einrichtung. Ein großer Raum bildet das Herz des Hauses, in dem verschiedene Bereiche ineinander übergehen. So grenzt das Esszimmer an das Wohnzimmer, wo sich auch eine kleine Arbeitsecke befindet. Weiter steht das Bett direkt gegenüber einer alten Badewanne. Stil, Farbe und Fantasie sind elegant kombiniert ohne die traditionellen Formen und Materialien aufzugeben.

Dimensions généreuses et conception linéaire horizontale toute en longueur caractérisent cette maison. Une véranda en bois blanc court le long de la façade turquoise et mène à la maison dotée d'une décoration aux couleurs vives. Le cœur de la demeure est une grande pièce, où différents espaces communiquent entre eux. La salle à manger jouxte le salon où se trouve un mini coin bureau. Un peu plus loin, le lit est placé juste en face d'une vieille baignoire. Style, couleur et fantaisie se mélangent avec élégance sans pour autant renoncer aux formes et matières traditionnelles.

Dimensiones generosas y amplias líneas horizontales son las señas de identidad de esta construcción. La veranda de madera blanca conduce a lo largo de la fachada color turquesa hacia el interior de la casa, decorada de forma colorista. Una enorme sala constituye el corazón de la vivienda, en el que confluyen diversos espacios de funciones variadas. Así, el comedor limita con el salón, que tiene un pequeño despacho en uno de sus rincones. Más allá, la cama descansa junto a una bañera antigua. Estilo, color y fantasía se combinan de forma elegante sin renunciar a formas y materiales tradicionales.

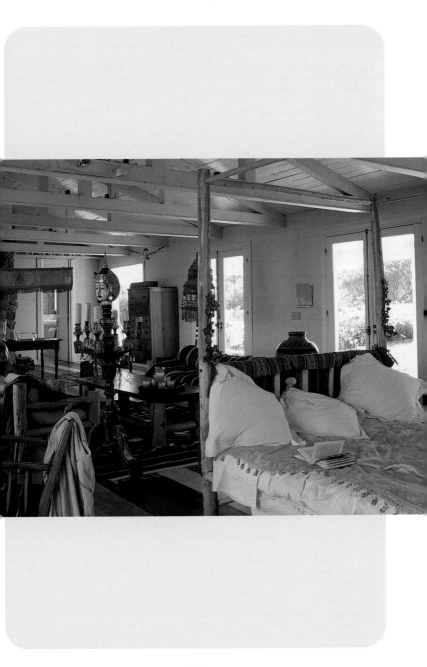

House of Wood

Architect: **Mario Connío**

Location: **Puerto Vallarta, Mexico**

Photos: **© Ricardo Labougle**

The architect's goal here was to create a house that is made of natural materials, is flooded with light and is a true haven away from it all. Composed of three units arrayed around a circular courtyard, the house is located on a small peninsula overlooking the sea by which it is almost completely surrounded. A round wooden deck visually reinforces the feeling of being in the middle of the ocean because the land just behind the garden looks as though it runs right into the water. The house has a spectacular panoramic view of the lagoon and, in the far distance, the horizon.

Natürliche Materialien, Licht und Unabhängigkeit waren die drei Leitgedanken, die den Architekten beim Bau dieses Hauses lenkten. Das Ensemble besteht aus drei kreisförmig angebrachten Einheiten, die durch einen runden Platz in der Mitte miteinander vereint sind. Das Haus ragt auf einer kleinen Halbinsel ins Wasser hinaus und ist dadurch zum größten Teil vom Ozean umgeben. Ein rundes Holzdeck verstärkt den optischen Effekt, der das Grundstück direkt hinter dem Garten scheinbar ins Meer fließen lässt. Das Auge wird durch die spektakuläre Lage mit Blicken in die Lagune und auf den weiten Horizont verwöhnt.

Matériaux naturels, lumière et indépendance sont les trois idées directrices suivies par l'architecte lors de la conception de cette maison. L'ensemble est composé de trois unités assemblées de manière circulaire, reliées entre elles par une place ronde au milieu. La maison avance au-dessus de la petite péninsule où elle est bâtie, surplombant ainsi l'océan qui l'encercle en grande partie. Un ponton rond en bois accentue l'illusion optique d'un terrain se jetant, juste au bout du jardin, directement dans la mer. L'emplacement spectaculaire avec la vue sur la lagune et l'horizon infini est un véritable régal visuel.

Materiales naturales, luz e independencia fueron los tres criterios que guiaron al arquitecto en la construcción de esta casa. El conjunto está compuesto de tres edificios circulares unidos por una plaza redonda situada en el centro. La construcción se alza en una pequeña península por lo que está prácticamente rodeada por el océano. Un tejado redondo de madera subraya el efecto óptico por el que parece que el solar fluye hacia el mar más allá del jardín. La vista se recrea así con las espectaculares panorámicas sobre la laguna que se extienden hasta el lejano horizonte.

Eastern
Hemisphere

House Tzaneen

Architect: **Ora Joubert & Thomas Gouws**

Location: **South Africa**

Photos: **© Graeme Borchers and Christoph Hoffmann**

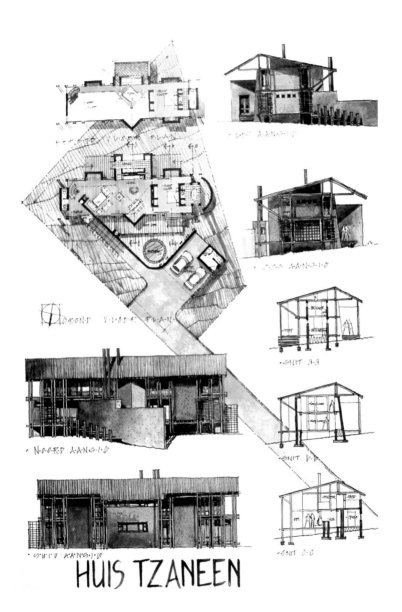

HUIS TZANEEN

In designing and building this house the owners placed great importance on adapting it to the heat, humidity and torrential rains that are characteristic of tropical climates. This explains why the Nothnagel-Deiner's home, like the vast majority of the homes in the area, uses light wood construction and reflective material for the roof, which also has a very large overhang. The terraces beneath this overhang are sometimes used as bedrooms. In addition, clean as a whistle copings and aerated closet doors minimize dampness and keep mildew at bay.

Die Bauherren Nothnagel-Deiner legten beim Bau ihres Hauses großen Wert darauf, dass es den klimatischen Bedingungen der Tropen – Hitze, Feuchtigkeit und schweren Platzregen – angepasst ist. Die meisten Häuser in der Umgebung sind daher mit einer leichten Holzkonstruktion und einem reflektierenden Material für das Dach ausgestattet, das außerdem weit überhängt. Auf die dadurch entstehenden großen, überdachten Terrassen werden zum Teil sogar die Schlafplätze verlegt. Desweiteren verringern sauber verputzte Mauerkronen und belüftete Schranktüren die Feuchtigkeit und vermeiden Schimmelbildung.

En construisant leur maison, les maîtres d'œuvre Nothnagel-Deiner ont attaché une grande importance à ce qu'elle soit adaptée aux conditions climatiques des tropiques – chaleur, humidité et pluies torrentielles brutales. C'est pour cela que la plupart des constructions environnantes sont des structures légères en bois avec des toitures équipées de matières réfléchissantes, dépassant largement la maison. Les terrasses spacieuses ainsi bien protégées sont utilisées en partie, pour y dormir. En outre, les couronnements de murs au revêtement impeccable et les portes d'armoires sont ventilées pour réduire le taux d'humidité et éviter la formation de moisissures.

Los propietarios Nothnagel-Deiner concedieron gran importancia a que la construcción de la casa se adaptara a las condiciones climáticas de los trópicos: calor, humedad y aguaceros. La mayoría de las edificaciones de la zona están formadas por una ligera estructura de madera y tienen tejados de materiales reflectores que suelen sobresalir ampliamente por encima de la planta del edificio. Las terrazas techadas que se forman debajo pueden servir incluso de dormitorio. Los remates limpiamente revocados y las puertas de los armarios con ventilación reducen la humedad y evitan, de esta manera, la formación de moho.

Aleenta

Architects: **Pandarat Indrapim, Simple Space Design Co. Ltd.**

Interior Design: **Paisarn Krusong, Simple Space Design Co. Ltd.**

Location: **Pranburi Beach, Thailand**

Photos: © **Focus 1 International Resources Co. Ltd.**

Aleenta, a name derived from the Sanskrit word for "worthwhile life", is located in Pranburi Beach, which is about a twenty minute drive south of Hua Hin making this home an ideal getaway retreat from the hurlyburly of Bangkok. The villa contains five rooms with ocean view and there are also three beach bungalows that have their own pool. The sundeck of the two-story main house with a second swimming pool affords a lovely view of the Gulf of Siam. In short, Aleenta is a little piece of heaven on the beach.

Der Name „Aleenta" kommt aus dem alten Sanskrit und bedeutet „lohnendes Leben". Aleenta ist in Pranburi Beach gelegen, ungefähr zwanzig Minuten südlich von Hua Hin, was es zu einem idealen Zufluchtsort vor Bangkok macht. Die Villa besteht aus fünf Zimmern mit Meerblick und drei Strandbungalows mit Pool. Auf dem Sonnendach des zweistöckigen Haupthauses kann man sich in einem weiteren Schwimmbad mit Blick auf den Golf von Siam erfrischen. Aleenta ist ein privates luxuriöses Strandbad zum Wohl-Fühlen.

Le nom « Aleenta » est tiré du sanskrit ancien et signifie « vie enrichissante ». Aleenta est situé sur la Pranburi Beach, à vingt minutes environ au sud de Hua Hin, ce qui en fait un lieu d'évasion idéal, aux portes de Bangkok. La villa comporte cinq chambres avec vue sur la mer et trois bungalows de plage dotés d'une piscine. Du solarium, situé au deuxième étage du bâtiment principal, on peut se rafraîchir dans une autre piscine et jouir de la vue sur le Golfe de Siam. Aleenta, petite plage privée luxueuse, est un îlot de bien-être.

El nombre de "Aleenta" proviene del sanscrito y significa "vida provechosa". Aleenta está situada en Pranburi Beach, a unos 20 minutos al sur de Hua Hin, un lugar ideal de refugio para los habitantes de Bangkok. La enorme casa tiene cinco habitaciones con vistas al mar y tres bungalows con piscina en la playa. En la azotea del edificio principal de dos pisos de altura hay otra piscina donde se puede contemplar panorámicas del golfo de Siam. Aleenta es una lujosa playa privada para disfrutar y relajarse.

Casa Sayang

Architects: **CSL Associates**
Location: **Kuala Lumpur, Malaysia**
Photos: © **CSL Associates**

The underlying architectural concept of Casa Sayang was to create an eminently liveable home open on all sides with a large swimming pool. Enthroned atop a steep hill, this semicircular villa has a fabulous panoramic view of Kuala Lumpur below. The master bedroom is located right at the top of the dwelling, much like an eagle's nest. It is accessable through a spiral staircase. Striking, decorative Asian objects delight the eye everywhere in this wooden palace. A waterfall, constructed to counteract the noise from the busy thoroughfare nearby, flows into a stream which empties into the swimming pool and jacuzzi.

Die Grundidee bestand darin, einen rund herum offenen, bewohnbaren Pavillon mit einem großen Swimming Pool zu entwerfen. Die halbkreisförmige Villa Sayang thront auf einem steilen Abhang und bietet dadurch eine herrliche Aussicht auf Kuala Lumpur. Das Schlafzimmer befindet sich, gleich einem Adlernest, ganz oben im First. Der Zugang führt über eine spiralförmige Treppe. Bemerkenswerte asiatische Dekorationsobjekte ergötzen das Auge auf jedem Weg durch dieses „Holzschloss". Um den Lärm der großen Straße akustisch zu überdecken, wurde ein Wasserfall konstruiert, der über ein Flüsschen in den Swimming Pool und den Whirlpool mündet.

Basée sur l'idée d'être un pavillon habitable, complètement ouvert avec une grande piscine, la Villa Sayang, semi-circulaire, trône sur un versant abrupt, offrant ainsi une vue superbe sur Kuala Lumpur. A l'instar d'un nid d'aigle, la chambre à coucher se trouve tout en haut
du faîte. L'entrée s'ouvre sur un escalier hélicoïdal. En déambulant dans ce « château de
bois », le regard est attiré par des objets de décoration asiatiques remarquables. La construction d'une cascade qui passe par un ruisseau vers la piscine pour déboucher sur le bain
à remous permet de couvrir le bruit de la grande artère.

La idea base era crear un pabellón habitable, abierto en la totalidad de sus lados y con una
enorme piscina. La Casa Sayang, en forma de media luna, se alza sobre un escarpado pre-
cipicio y ofrece, de esta manera, una extraordinaria panorámica sobre Kuala Lumpur. El dormitorio, como si se tratara de un nido de águilas, se ubica en la parte superior. Se accede
a él por una escalera en espiral. Extraordinarios objetos decorativos orientales recrean la
vista por doquier en este "palacio de madera". Para paliar el ruido de la carretera cercana,
se construyó una cascada sobre un riachuelo, cuyas aguas desembocan en la piscina
con jacuzzi.

Eu House

Architects: **CSL Associates**
Location: **Kuala Lumpur, Malaysia**
Photos: © **CSL Associates**

This house stands on a 26,000 square foot lot in Damansara, a small suburb of Kuala Lumpur. A hilltop home in the foothills of the mountains, it affords residents a breathtaking panoramic view of the city and valley below. Architectonically, the house is structured around its central staircase, a vertical element that both separates and links the various rooms. This staircase gives way to a rooftop structure that is reminiscent of an oversized round fin. The kitchen and dining area are on the ground floor while the upper level contains the three bedrooms. The guest house set off from the main house and is linked to it by a covered walkway.

Das Haus steht auf einem Grundstück von 2.440 m² in Damansara, einem kleinen Vorort von Kuala Lumpur. Auf einem Bergvorsprung gelegen bietet es eine fantastische Aussicht auf das Tal der Stadt. Die zentrale Treppe bildet die Mittelachse der Konstruktion, ein vertikales Element, das die Räume gliedert und gleichzeitig verbindet. Sie endet in einer Dachkonstruktion, die wie eine große, runde Flosse wirkt. Im Erdgeschoss befinden sich Küche und Esszimmer und in der oberen Etage liegen die drei Schlafzimmer. Der Gästepavillon ist etwas abgelegen und durch einen überdachten Fußweg mit dem Haupthaus verbunden.

Cette maison se trouve à Damansara, un petit faubourg de Kuala Lumpur, sur un terrain de 2.440 m². Située sur un promontoire montagneux, elle offre une vue magnifique sur la vallée et la ville. L'escalier central constitue la ligne médiane de la construction. Elément vertical, il structure et relie en même temps les pièces et aboutit sous une toiture qui fait penser à une immense nageoire ronde. Le rez-de-chaussée abrite la cuisine et la salle à manger et l'étage supérieur les trois chambres à coucher. Le pavillon des invités, un peu en retrait, est relié à la maison principale par un chemin recouvert d'un toit.

Esta casa se edificó sobre un terreno de 2.440 m² en Damansara, un pequeño barrio a las afueras de Kuala Lumpur. Situada en el saliente de una montaña, ofrece una fantástica panorámica del valle donde está ubicada la ciudad. Una escalera central conforma el eje medio de la construcción, un elemento vertical que articula las habitaciones y, al mismo tiempo, las comunica entre sí, y finaliza en un tejado cuya similitud recuerda a la enorme y redondeada aleta de un pez. En la planta baja se concentran la cocina y el comedor, mientras que el piso superior acoge los tres dormitorios. El pabellón de los huéspedes permanece un poco retirado y se comunica con la casa principal a través de un camino techado.

Nilly House

Architects: **CSL Associates**
Location: **Kuala Lumpur, Malaysia**
Photos: © **CSL Associates**

Nilly House is a two-story bungalow in the Kuala Lumpur suburb of Petaling Jaya. It is built according to the Kampong school of architecture whereby houses are clustered around a central community area. This concept has been applied here to a single family dwelling in which the swimming pool serves as the main gathering place. The generously proportioned pool is located very close to the house and half of it is roofed in order to cool the hot outdoor air before it has a chance to enter the house. The villa is virtually devoid of interior dividing walls which enables air currents to ventilate the open space more easily.

Das Nilly Haus ist ein zweistöckiger Bungalow in Petaling Jaya, einem Wohngebiet am Stadtrand von Kuala Lumpur. Es entstand nach dem „Kampong-Konzept", das Häuser um einen zentralen Gemeinschaftsplatz gruppiert. Dieses Konzept wurde hier auf eine Familie ausgerichtet: der zentrale Bereich ist der Swimming Pool, an dem man zusammenkommen kann. Das große Becken befindet sich sehr nah am Haus und ist halb überdacht, sodass es die heiße Luft erst abkühlt, bevor sie in das Haus eindringen kann. Die Villa hat fast keine Innenwände und ermöglicht den Luftströmen, den offenen Raum zu belüften.

La maison Nilly, bungalow à deux étages, est située à Petaling Jaya, une zone résidentielle sur la périphérie de Kuala Lumpur. Elle a été conçue d'après le « concept du Kampong » : rassembler les maisons autour d'une place commune centrale. Ici, cette conception a été adaptée à une famille : l'espace central commun est la piscine, où l'on peut se réunir. Le grand bassin très proche de la maison, à moitié recouvert, permet de refroidir l'air chaud avant qu'il ne pénètre dans la maison. La villa est presque dépourvue de cloisons laissant ainsi les courants d'air circuler pour aérer l'espace à vivre ouvert.

La casa Nilly es un bungalow de dos pisos situado en Petaling Jaya, una zona residencial a la afueras de Kuala Lumpur. Se concibió según el concepto "Kampong", que agrupa varias casas en torno a una plaza central común. Este modelo urbanístico se aplicó a las necesidades de una familia muy particular; consideró la piscina como el principal lugar de reunión, que llega casi hasta la casa y está semitechada, de forma que el aire caliente se enfría antes de que penetre en el edificio. La casa apenas tiene tabiques interiores, lo que permite que las corrientes de aire ventilen el diáfano espacio.

Precima House

Architects: **CSL Associates**
Location: **Kuala Lumpur, Malaysia**
Photos: © **CSL Associates**

Precima House was designed for two European bachelors who had spent the previous fifteen years living in various parts of southeast Asia. Since both men value their privacy, the architect had to come up with a design that basically provides for two separate dwellings. The resulting semicircular structure encompasses a swimming pool, making it and the adjoining patio—this dwelling's main gathering place—the centerpiece of the house. Both wings contain master bedrooms, each of which has a fabulous ensuite bathroom from which, upon awakening in the morning, the residents can step directly out into the pool area for a refreshing swim.

Dieses Haus wurde für zwei Junggesellen aus Europa entworfen, die bereits in den vergangenen 15 Jahren in unterschiedlichen Regionen Südostasiens gelebt hatten. Da beide ihre Privatsphäre schätzen, mussten praktisch zwei Häuser in einem geschaffen werden. Der Bau mit seiner halbrunden Form umschließt den Swimming Pool und macht ihn gemeinsam mit der dahinter liegenden Terrasse, die gleichzeitig der Hauptaufenthaltsbereich der Bewohner ist, zum Herzen des Hauses. Die Schlafzimmer befinden sich in den beiden Flügeln, mit einem jeweils wunderschön integrierten Badezimmer. Von hier aus kann man morgens nach dem Aufstehen direkt in den Pool springen.

Cette maison a été conçue pour deux célibataires européens ayant vécu les dernières quinze années dans différentes régions de l'Asie du sud-est. Attachés l'un et l'autre à leur sphère privée, il a fallu pratiquement créer deux maisons en une. La construction en demi-cercle épouse la forme de la piscine et l'intègre à la terrasse en retrait, lieu de séjour principal des habitants, au cœur de la maison. Les chambres à coucher installées dans les deux ailes sont dotées de splendides salles de bains intégrées. De là, dès le réveil, on peut plonger directement dans la piscine.

Esta casa fue diseñada para dos solteros europeos que en los últimos 15 años habían vivido en diferentes regiones del sudeste asiático. Debido a que ambos querían salvaguardar su esfera privada, se levantaron dos casas en un mismo espacio. La construcción de forma semicircular rodea la piscina y la abre hacia la terraza posterior, condicionada también como sala de estar, y constituye el corazón de la casa. Los dormitorios se sitúan en ambas alas de la vivienda, cada uno con un precioso cuarto de baño integrado. La perfecta ubicación de las habitaciones permite que los propietarios se levanten y se dirijan directamente a la piscina.

Lim Residence

Architects: **CSL Associates**
Location: **Kuala Lumpur, Malaysia**
Photos: © **CSL Associates**

Located on the outskirts of Kuala Lumpur, Lim Residence was originally constructed in 1975 and then underwent numerous remodelings and renovations until being completed in 1995. This unique structure serves not only as a home but also as a laboratory for the ideas of the architect Jimmy Lim, who spends much of his time contemplating the challenges and untapped potential of tropical home design. The house is made of 80 percent recycled materials, mainly wood from defunct buildings. The dwelling affords all the advantages of natural ventilation and in many respects is a classic prototype of tropical architecture.

Die Lim Residenz liegt in einem kleinen Randgebiet von Kuala Lumpur. Der Originalbungalow wurde 1975 gebaut und nach mehreren Renovierungsarbeiten 1995 fertiggestellt. Dieses einzigartige Gebäude dient nicht nur als Heim, sondern auch als Experimentierstätte des Architekten Jimmy Lim. Hier entstehen neue Ideen und es wird über Herausforderungen und Grenzen der tropischen Architektur gebrütet. Das Haus besteht zu 80% aus wiederverwerteten Materialien anderer Gebäude und ist fast ausschließlich aus Holz gebaut. Es bietet alle Vorteile natürlicher Ventilation, und man kann sagen, dass es einen Prototyp tropischer Architektur darstellt.

La résidence Lim se situe dans une petite banlieue de Kuala Lumpur. Ce bungalow original construit en 1975, a été terminé en 1995 après maints travaux de restauration. Cet édifice, unique en son genre, n'est pas seulement le logis de l'architecte Jimmy Lim, mais aussi son lieu d'expérimentation d'où fusent de nouvelles idées, des réflexions sur les défis et les limites de l'architecture tropicale. La maison est réalisée pour 80% à partir de matériaux de récupération en provenance d'autres bâtiments. Presque uniquement en bois, elle offre tous les avantages de la ventilation naturelle. On peut dire que c'est un prototype de l'architecture tropicale.

La residencia Lim está situada en un pequeño barrio en las afueras de Kuala Lumpur. El bungalow original se construyó en 1975 y, tras varias reformas, se finalizó en 1995. Este extraordinario edificio no solamente es el hogar del arquitecto Jimmy Lim, sino también su taller de experimentos. En este lugar concibe sus nuevas ideas y desarrolla soluciones para los retos y límites de la arquitectura tropical. La casa está construida con un 80% de materiales reciclados, principalmente de madera de antiguas construcciones. Ofrece las ventajas de una ventilación natural y, en muchos aspectos, es prototipo de la arquitectura tropical.

323

Sadesh House

Architects: **Bedmar & Shi Pte. Ltd.**

Location: **Kuala Lumpur, Malaysia**

Photos: © **Ernesto Bedmar**

Sadesh House consists of three structures in a horseshoe configuration. Two of the three units have two floors and the third unit is used as a foyer as well as a guest house. A bridge leads to the bedroom wing, which is separated from the other units by a high stone wall whose deftly sculpted openings allow residents to see into the landscaped inner courtyard on the other side. The compellingly lovely garden separates the entryway from the residential wing, which contains the living room and other common areas. The pool has been placed right alongside the house in order to cool the thermally challenging tropical air.

Das Sadesh Haus umfasst drei Gebäude, deren Grundriss in U-Form angelegt ist. Zwei der drei Einheiten haben zwei Etagen und das Dritte dient als Foyer und Gästehaus. Über eine kleine Brücke gelangt man in den Schlaftrakt, der durch eine große Steinmauer von den restlichen Gebäuden getrennt ist. Es sind kunstvolle Öffnungen in die Mauer eingearbeitet, sodass man auf den grünen Innenhof blicken kann. Der idyllische Garten teilt den Eingangsbereich von dem Wohnblock gegenüber, in dem sich Wohnzimmer und Aufenthaltsbereich befinden. Der Pool wurde direkt entlang des Hauses gebaut, um die tropische Luft abzukühlen.

La résidence Sadesh comprend trois bâtiments, conçus en forme de U. Deux des trois unités sont à deux étages et la troisième fait office de foyer et de maison d'invités. Un petit pont mène à la partie nuit, séparée du reste des bâtiments par un mur de pierre. Des ouvertures pratiquées dans le mur de manière artistique, permettent d'apercevoir la cour intérieure, nid de verdure. Le jardin idyllique sépare l'entrée de l'édifice vis à vis, où se trouvent salon et pièce à vivre. La piscine, implantée le long de la maison, permet de rafraîchir l'air tropical .

La casa Sadesh está formada por tres edificios con planta en U. Dos de las tres unidades son de dos alturas, y la tercera sirve de vestíbulo y alojamiento para los invitados. A través de un pequeño puente, se accede a la zona de dormitorio, separada del resto de la construcción por un grueso muro de piedra. La pared muestra aberturas inteligentemente colocadas que permiten disfrutar de las vistas hacia el verde patio interior. El idílico jardín separa la zona de entrada del bloque de vivienda situado justo enfrente, donde se encuentra la sala y otras estancias de recreo. La piscina está construida a lo largo de la casa para refrigerar el aire tropical.

House in Holland Road

Architects: **Guz architects**

Location: **Singapore**

Photos: © **Luca Tettoni & Guz architects**

This house on old Holland Road is a prime example of timeless and environmentally friendly architecture. The house harmonizes with the prevailing climate and integrates elements from the Arts & Crafts movement. The entire three-level entranceway constitutes a large ventilation system. The guest house is strategically positioned under an ancient tree and a kind of grotto has been built right underneath to keep the swimming pool area cool. The rooftop gardens not only enhance the ambience of the upstairs bedrooms but also keep the rooms cool and create a link between the upper floors and the natural environment.

Das Haus an der alten Holland Road ist ein sehr gutes Beispiel für zeitloses und umweltfreundliches Design. Es wird dem herrschenden Klima gerecht und übernimmt Elemente aus der Arts & Crafts-Bewegung. Der gesamte dreistöckige Eingangsbereich stellt ein großes Ventilationssystem dar. Im Garten wurde der Gästepavillon unter einem alten Baum platziert, und direkt darunter wurde in einer Art Grotte zur Abkühlung der Swimming Pool gebaut. Dachgärten bereichern die oberen Schlafzimmer. Sie dienen sowohl dazu, die unteren Räume kühl zu halten als auch dazu, die oberen Etagen mit der Natur zu verbinden.

La maison sur l'ancienne Holland Road est un bon exemple de design intemporel, respec-
tueux de l'environnement. Adaptée au climat local, elle reprend des éléments du mouvement Arts & Crafts. L'entrée qui s'étend sur trois étages, est un modèle imposant de système de ventilation. Au jardin, le pavillon des invités est placé sous un vieil arbre. Juste
au-dessous, il y a une sorte de grotte construite pour abriter la piscine, et se rafraîchir. Les
chambres à coucher du haut sont dotées de jardins en terrasse, sources de fraîcheur et
liens entre les étages supérieurs et la nature.

Esta residencia del antiguo Holland Road es un buen ejemplo de diseño atemporal y de respeto con el entorno natural. La construcción se adapta al clima y adopta elementos del movimiento arts & crafts. La zona de entrada, de una altura total de tres pisos, actúa como un
enorme sistema de ventilación. En el jardín se levantó una pérgola bajo un árbol centenario
y, justo debajo, una especie de gruta fue construida para conservar fresca la zona de la piscina. Los dormitorios del piso superior se abren a terrazas ajardinadas que mantienen el ambiente confortable de las estancias inferiores e integra los pisos de arriba con la naturaleza.

338

Leedon Park

Architects: **Guz architects**
Location: **Singapore**
Photos: **© Luca Tettoni & Guz architects**

This architecture of this residence, which was built in 1930, was influenced by the Arts & Crafts movement and has a lovely, warm atmosphere that mitigates the heaviness of this massive structure. The house's floor plan in the form of an H is anchored to the ground, and the materials used were carefully selected to ensure that all elements blend in harmoniously with each other. For example, the roof's cedar shingles are of a piece with the trees in the yard whose lengthwise pool constitutes a separate element. Somewhat screened off from and behind the pool is a gazebo which is a lovely place to relax.

Das von der Arts & Crafts-Bewegung inspirierte Wohnhaus aus dem Jahre 1930 ist mit einer behaglichen Atmosphäre erfüllt, die die Schwere dieses sehr großen Hauses mildert. Sein H-förmiger Grundriss ist fest mit dem Boden verankert, und die Materialien wurden so ausgesucht, dass alle Einheiten harmonisch miteinander verschmelzen. Das Dach wurde mit Zedernholz eingekleidet, um es mit dem Garten in Einklang zu bringen. Der Pool ist länglich geschnitten und wurde als unabhängige Einheit im Garten angelegt. Dahinter befindet sich, etwas abgeschirmt, ein Pavillon, der zur Entspannung einlädt.

L'immeuble des années trente, inspiré du mouvement Arts & Crafts est empreint d'une atmosphère agréable qui atténue la lourdeur de cette immense demeure. Le plan en forme de H est bien ancré au sol, et les éléments ont été choisis afin que chaque unité s'enchevêtre harmonieusement l'une dans l'autre. La toiture est recouverte de bois de cèdre, pour être à l'unisson avec le jardin. La piscine toute en longueur est installée dans le jardin, indépendante de la maison. Un pavillon, quelque peu en retrait, invite à la détente.

Esta casa, inspirada por el movimiento arts & crafts de la década de los treinta, tiene un ambiente agradable que suaviza la pesadez del enorme edificio. Su planta en forma de H está firmemente arraigada en el suelo, y los materiales que se utilizaron para su construcción se escogieron de tal forma que se funden en un todo armonioso. El tejado, recubierto de madera de cedro, se integra en el entorno natural. La piscina, de forma alargada, fue emplazada en el jardín como elemento independiente. Detrás de ella, una pérgola protegida invita a la relajación y al descanso.

344

Oei Tiong Ham Park

Architects: **Guz architects**

Location: **Singapore**

Photos: © **Luca Tettoni & Guz architects**

This house is inhabited by an extended family and has extra rooms for other family members in two separate wings that are linked by a central courtyard. In order to accommodate the desired spatial configuration, the extensive living space had to be fit onto a relatively small piece of property in such a way that the building didn't end up looking too bulky. This is why the architect decided to include a central courtyard, which also has the virtue of providing good natural ventilation. Gardens were planted on the terraces on each floor, creating a sense of intimacy throughout the living space while at the same time their lush vegetation keeps the rooms below cool.

Diese Residenz dient als Wohnsitz für eine Großfamilie mit Unterbringungsmöglichkeiten für mehrere Familienmitglieder in zwei separaten Flügeln, die durch einen zentralen Patio miteinander verbunden sind. Um den Anforderungen der Raumkonzeption gerecht zu werden, musste die weitläufige Wohnfläche auf dem relativ kleinen Grundstück so ausgerichtet werden, dass das Gebäude nicht zu massig wirkt. Aus diesem Grund wurde im Herzen des Hauses ein Hof entworfen, der zugleich für erfrischenden Durchzug sorgt. Eine Reihe Terrassengärten wurden in allen Stockwerken angelegt. Sie schaffen Intimität für jede Wohneinheit und halten durch die dichte Bepflanzung die darunter liegenden Räume kühl.

Cette résidence prévue pour une grande famille et l'accueil de plusieurs de ses membres est conçue en deux ailes séparées, reliées entre elles par un patio central. Pour répondre aux contraintes de la conception de l'espace, il a fallu organiser une grande surface habitable sur un terrain relativement petit, afin que l'ensemble architectural ne soit pas trop massif. La solution a été de concevoir une cour, au cœur de la maison, source génératrice de courants d'air frais. Une série de jardins en terrasse festonne chaque étage préservant ainsi l'intimité de chaque unité d'habitation et grâce à la densité des plantes, la fraîcheur des pièces au-dessous.

Esta casa, residencia de una familia numerosa, ofrece alojamiento a sus miembros en dos alas separadas y comunicadas entre sí por un patio central. Para responder a las necesidades de la concepción espacial, se logró integrar una amplia superficie habitable sobre un solar relativamente pequeño sin que la construcción resultase demasiado compacta e imponente. De este modo, se diseñó el patio interior que, además, proporciona ventilación al edificio. Todos los pisos poseen terrazas ajardinadas para dar intimidad a cada unidad de la vivienda y, al mismo tiempo, mantener frescas las estancias inferiores.

Villa Kirana

Architects: **P.T. Wijaya Tribwana International**
Location: **Bali, Indonesia**
Photos: © **P.T. Wijaya Tribwana International**

Villa Kirana, a vacation home belonging to an Australian family, is located on the Ayung river in rural Ubud, Bali, surrounded by terraced rice paddies and coconut palms. In designing this house Made Wijaya—who acted as architect, interior architect and landscape architect—was inspired by Arne Hasselquist's David Bowie house in Mustique, on which Wijaya himself also worked in 1985. The villa consists of a series of open dwellings set amidst romantic tropical water gardens which also act as a cooling system. Berber rugs from Morocco create colorful accents, while the house's doors and windows are adorned with folk art.

Die Villa Kirana ist das Ferienhaus einer australischen Familie und liegt in der ländlichen Gegend von Ubud, umgeben von Reisfeldterrassen und Kokospalmen am Fluss Ayung. Der Architekt, Innenarchitekt und Landschaftsplaner Made Wijaya ließ sich von Arne Hasselquists David-Bowie-Haus auf Mustique inspirieren, an dem er selbst 1985 mitwirkte. Die Villa besteht aus einer Serie offener Pavillons inmitten von romantischen, tropischen Wassergärten, die als Kühlsysteme einen zusätzlichen Zweck erfüllen. Marokkanische Berberteppiche setzen Farbakzente und die Türen und Fenster sind mit volkstümlicher Kunst verziert.

La villa Kirana, villégiature d'une famille australienne se situe dans la campagne d'Ubud, entourée de rizières en terrasse et de cocotiers le long de la rivière Ayung. Made Wijaya, architecte, paysagiste et architecte d'intérieur s'est inspiré de la maison de David-Bowie par Arne Hasselquist sur l'île Moustique, à la conception de laquelle il a d'ailleurs participé en 1985. La villa est composée d'une série de pavillons ouverts au milieu de jardins aquatiques tropicaux romantiques, conçus pour refroidir l'atmosphère. Des tapis berbères marocains ajoutent des touches de couleurs. Portes et fenêtres sont décorées d'artisanat régional.

Villa Kirana, situada en la zona campestre de Ubud y rodeada de terrazas de arroz y cocoteros a orillas del río Ayung, es la residencia donde veranea una familia australiana. Para este proyecto, el arquitecto, interiorista y jardinero paisajista Made Wijaya se inspiró en la casa que Arne Hasselquist erigió para David Bowie en Mustique en 1985, y en la que él mismo colaboró. La mansión está compuesta de una serie de pabellones situados en medio de románticos jardines tropicales llenos de canales y fuentes, con el objetivo de refrescar el ambiente. Las alfombras bereberes ponen una nota de color al paisaje, y las puertas y ventanas están engalanadas con artesanía popular.

Elevations

Villa Angsa

Architects: **P.T. Wijaya Tribwana International**
Location: **Bali, Indonesia**
Photos: © **P.T. Wijaya Tribwana International**

Villa Angsa is located in Mertasari-Sanur, Bali, opposite its "sister villa" Bebek, where P.T. Wijaya and his team have their offices. This L-shaped structure is set on an 8,500 square foot lot. A simple, wooden staircase of light construction leads to the first floor which accommodates the bedrooms and community areas. Wijaya's large paintings infuse the Balinese "open air living room" with a theatrical ambience and at the same time provide privacy by screening the house from the one next door. A small guest house equipped with a kitchen is located by the pool in the yard, away from the main house.

Die Villa Angsa liegt in Mertasari-Sanur, Bali gegenüber Ihrer „Schwester-Villa" Bebek, dem Büro des Architektenteams P.T. Wijaya. Die Villa Angsa wurde in L-Form auf das 800 m² große Grundstück gebaut. Eine schlichte, leichte Holztreppe führt hinauf in den ersten Stock, wo sich die Schlafzimmer und der Aufenthaltsbereich befinden. Wijayas große Kunstbilder verleihen dem balinesischen „Open-air-Wohnzimmer" eine theatralische Atmosphäre und dienen gleichzeitig dazu, die Blicke der Nachbarn abzuschirmen. Ein kleines Gästehaus mit Küche liegt am Pool, separat vom Hauptgebäude im Garten.

La villa Angsa est à Mertasari-Sanur, Bali, en face de la « villa-sœur » Bebek, bureau du groupe d'architectes P.T. Wijaya. La villa Angsa est construite en forme de L sur un grand terrain de 800 m². Un escalier de bois, épuré et léger, mène au premier étage, où se trouvent la chambre à coucher et les pièces à vivre. Les grands tableaux d'art de Wijaya confèrent « au séjour à ciel ouvert » balinais une ambiance théâtrale et servent en même temps à protéger du regard indiscret des voisins. La piscine est dotée d'une petite maison d'invités avec cuisine, séparée du bâtiment principal par un jardin.

Villa Angsa se erige en Mertasari-Sanur, en Bali, frente a su "villa gemela" Bebek, oficina del equipo de arquitectos P.T. Wijaya. La casa se construyó en forma de U sobre un solar de 800 m². Una sencilla y ligera escalera conduce hasta el primer piso donde se encuentran los dormitorios y la zona de estar. Los grandes cuadros de Wijaya, colocados a modo de bastidores, dan a esta peculiar sala de estar balinesa al aire libre de un aspecto teatral, y sirven a su vez para protegerla de las miradas vecinas. Situada en el jardín, al lado de la piscina, se alza una casita para invitados equipada con cocina, independiente del edificio principal.

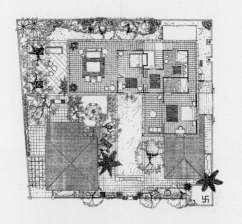

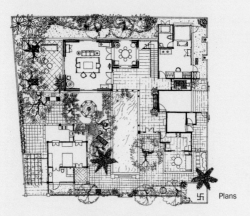

Plans

Bamboo House

Architect: **Putu Suarsa**
Location: **Sanur, Indonesia**
Photos: **© Reto Guntli**

Sanur's idyllic island atmosphere persuaded native Australians Walter and Hinke Zieck that they just had to live here. Formerly a prize winning fashion designer, Hinke became an artist and interior designer. When she is not busy repainting the front door of the house or the kitchen table, she paints at her easel. Her creativity is palable throughout the house. Amazingly, parades of frogs and other wildlife make ritual evening visits to the house, where they are welcome guests. Bamboo House was constructed by Balinese bamboo baron Putu Suarsai, whose clients also include Mick Jagger, Mario Ferrari and David Bowie.

Die paradiesische Atmosphäre der Insel verführte die gebürtigen Australier Walter und Hinke Zieck dazu, sich hier niederzulassen. Die ehemals preisgekrönte Modedesignerin arbeitet heute als Innenarchitektin und Künstlerin. Wenn sie nicht gerade die Eingangstür neu streicht oder dem Küchentisch einen neuen Farbton verpasst, malt sie an ihrer Staffelei. Ihr kreativer Geist ist überall in diesem offenen Heim spürbar. Überraschenderweise hüpfen ganze Froschparaden bei ihrem abendlichen Ritual durch das Haus, und auch andere Besucher aus dem Tierreich sind willkommen. Erbaut wurde Bamboo House vom balinesischen Bambus-Baron Putu Suarsai, der auch Mick Jagger, Mario Ferrari und David Bowie zu seinen Klienten zählt.

Walter et Hinke Zieck, australiens de souche, séduits par l'atmosphère paradisiaque de l'île, s'y sont installés. L'ex-styliste primée travaille aujourd'hui en tant qu'architecte d'intérieur et artiste. Quand elle n'est pas en train de repeindre la porte d'entrée ou de changer la teinte de la table de cuisine, elle est devant son chevalet. Cette maison ouverte respire l'esprit créatif de son hôtesse. Il ne faut pas s'étonner, au crépuscule, de voir des ribambelles de grenouilles faire leur promenade rituelle à travers la maison où d'autres visiteurs du monde animal sont les bienvenus. La Bamboo House est l'œuvre du balinais Putu Suarsai, baron du bambou, qui compte aussi au nombre de ses clients Mick Jagger, Mario Ferrari et David Bowie.

La atmósfera paradisiaca de la isla llevó a los australianos Walter e Hinke Zieck a establecerse en ella. Actualmente, la antaño prestigiosa diseñadora de moda trabaja como artista y arquitecta de interiores. Cuando no se encuentra dando una capa de pintura a la puerta de entrada o un nuevo color a la mesa de la cocina, trabaja en su caballete. Su creativo espíritu es presente en este hogar abierto. Como curiosidad, ejércitos de ranas cruzan a saltos la vivienda en un sorprendente ritual nocturno; otros visitantes del reino animal son también bienvenidos. Bamboo House fue levantada por el balinés Putu Suarsai, barón del bambú, quien tiene clientes como Mick Jagger, Mario Ferrari y David Bowie.

Villa Desa Kilana

Interior Design: **By the residents**
Location: **Sanur, Indonesia**
Photos: © **Reto Guntli**

Villa Desa Kilana is located in an exclusive area of Batujimbar on the island of Sanur, only a stone's throw away from the beach. The villa is comprised of four lovely structures, an elegant garden graced with ponds and numerous terraces. The central structure with its "wantilan" (a straw roof that provides ventilation) is located right next to the pool. The roofs set on stilts cool the open living area which the owner Michelle Han has decorated stylishly. The living area also contains a wet bar and a dining room, the latter on a somewhat raised level. A bridge across a water lily pond leads to the other structures in the exotic garden, including the master bedroom, a guest room, a tv room and a studio.

Die Villa Desa Kilana befindet sich in einem privaten Viertel von Batujimbar in Sanur, nur zehn Schritte vom Strand entfernt. Sie besteht aus vier geschmackvollen Gebäuden, einem eleganten Garten mit Teichen und mehreren Terrassen. Der Hauptbau mit einem sogenannten „Wantilan" (Strohdach zur offenen Ventilation) wurde auf den Swimming Pool ausgerichtet. Die aufgestelzten Dächer beschirmen den offenen Wohnbereich, den die Besitzerin Michelle Han stilvoll eingerichtet hat. Hier befindet sich eine Bar und ein etwas höher gelegenes Esszimmer. Eine Brücke über einen Seerosenteich führt zu den anderen Teilen des Ensembles im exotischen Garten. Sie beherbergen die Schlaf- und Gästezimmer sowie auch Arbeits- und Fernsehzimmer.

La Villa Desa Kilana, située dans un quartier privé de Batujimbar à Sanur, n'est qu'à quelques pas de la plage. Elle est constituée de quatre bâtiments réalisés avec beaucoup de goût, d'un élégant jardin agrémenté d'étangs et de plusieurs terrasses. Le bâtiment principal doté d'un « Wantilan » (toiture de paille pour ventilation ouverte) a été orienté vers la piscine. Les toits sur pilotis protègent la pièce à vivre ouverte, dont l'agencement stylé est l'œuvre de la propriétaire, Michelle Han. Cet espace est pourvu d'un bar et d'une salle à manger légèrement surélevée. Un pont jeté au-dessus d'un étang de nénuphars rejoint les autres parties de l'ensemble au milieu d'un jardin exotique. Elles abritent les chambres à coucher et d'invités ainsi que le bureau et la salle de télévision.

Villa Desa Kilana se encuentra en un barrio privado de Batujimbar, en Sanur, muy próxima a la playa. Se compone de cuatro preciosos edificios, un elegante jardín con estanques y varias terrazas. La casa principal con su "wantilan" (tejado de paja que proporciona ventilación) está ubicada justo al lado de la piscina. Los tejados levantados cobijan la zona abierta del salón, decorada con estilo por la propietaria Michelle Han. Esta estancia alberga el bar y un comedor ligeramente elevado con respecto al nivel del suelo. Un puente cruza el estanque de nenúfares y conduce hasta las otras piezas del conjunto repartidas por el exótico jardín, donde están los dormitorios y la habitación de huéspedes, así como el despacho y el salón de la televisión.

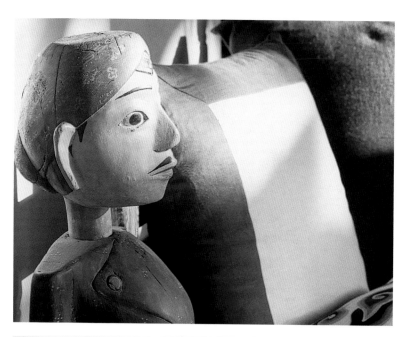

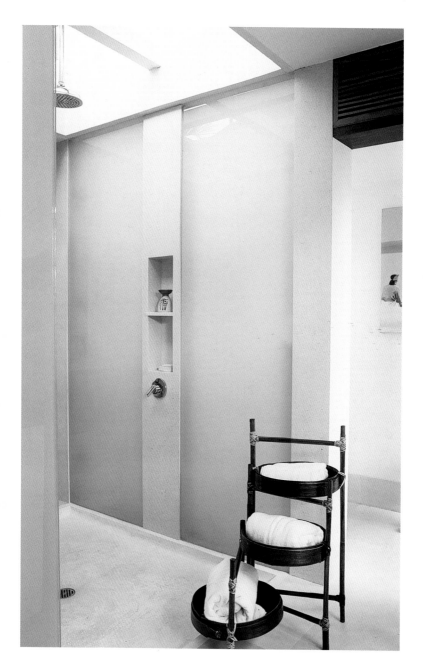

Kelekele

Architects: **Architects Pacific**
Location: **Wakaya Island, Fiji**
Photos: © **Architects Pacific**

"Kelekele", which is Fijian for "anchorage", was built in 1985 for the singer Glenn Shorrock, his wife Jo and their friends Lionel and Jody Hunt. Both families wanted a vacation home that would allow for plenty of privacy but would also have spaces that could be shared in common. The resulting design consists of three rounds structures all of which have a breathtaking panoramic view of the reef that encircles the island of Wakaya and forms the entrance to the lagoon. The "round house," as the residents call the living room, has the best view. The undersides of the conical thatched straw roofs are decorated with snail shells and coconut fibre weavings.

„Kelekele" bedeutet „Ankerplatz" auf Fidschianisch. Das Haus wurde 1985 für den Sänger Glenn Shorrock, seine Frau Jo und ihre Freunde Lionel und Jody Hunt gebaut. Der Wunsch beider Familien war ein Ferienhaus. Es sollte so aufgeteilt werden, dass sie ihre jeweilige Intimsphäre genießen und trotzdem einen Gemeinschaftsraum teilen könnten. Das Ergebnis sind drei runde Gebäude, die eine atemberaubende Aussicht auf das Riff haben, das die Insel Wakaya umringt und den Eingang zur Lagune bildet. Das „runde Haus", so heißt das Wohnzimmer, hat die beste Aussicht. Die kegelförmigen Dächer sind aus Stroh und von innen mit Webkunst aus Kokosnussfasern und Schneckenhäusern verziert.

Aux îles Fidji, « Kelekele » signifie « mouillage ». Cette maison a été construite en 1985 pour le chanteur Glenn Shorrock, son épouse Jo et ses amis Lionel et Jody Hunt. Les deux familles souhaitaient une maison de vacances. La conception devait préserver les sphères d'intimités respectives tout en gardant une pièce commune. Il en résulta trois bâtiments circulaires, avec une vue à couper le souffle sur le Riff qui entoure l'île Wakaya et donne accès à la lagune. La « maison ronde » ou salon, offre la plus belle vue. Les toits en forme de quille sont en paille. A l'intérieur, ils sont parés d'un tissage artistique où s'entrelacent fibres de noix de coco et coquillages.

El término "kelekele" significa "fondeadero" en el idioma autóctono de las islas Fiji. La casa se construyó en 1985 para el cantante Glenn Shorrock, su mujer Jo y sus amigos Lionel y Jody Hunt. La idea era disponer de una casa para pasar las vacaciones, donde cada pareja pudiera disfrutar plenamente de intimidad pero con zonas comunes para compartir. El resultado consiste en tres edificios redondos con una impresionante vista del arrecife que rodea la isla Wakaya y forma la entrada a la laguna. La "casa redonda", como se llama el salón, posee la mejor panorámica de los tres. Los tejados en forma de cono son de paja y están recubiertos en su interior de un trenzado de fibra de coco y caracolas.